C000186913

Everyone at some point
they are heading in life. I
find the answers they a
common sense, and wit
book poses questions that will enable you to find the
guidance you need. At times we all need a friend with the
right answers. Shirley's book is that friend.

—Anne Jirsch

Author of *The Future Is Yours: Introducing Future Life Progression—*
The Dynamic Technique that Reveals Your Destiny

12 Words is a remarkable book where Shirley shares many
simple tools that can guide us through our daily lives. I
love how it is so creative, informative, and uplifting. I am
sure it will bring about profound change for any reader. It
truly is a must read.

—Eamonn Holmes

Anchor of *Sky News Sunrise* and presenter of ITV's *This Morning*

Shirley offers a creative and practical new twist to playing the game of life, achieving more and being happy. *12
Words* is a wise and inspiring book.

—Marci Shimoff

Author of *Happy for No Reason*
and *Chicken Soup for the Woman's Soul*

Pick up a copy of Shirley Palmer's book, *12 Words*, and I promise that you will find some exceptional ideas that you can put to work in improving your life and happiness each and every day.

—Mary Morrissey
International speaker, author, founder
and owner of Life Mastery Institute

12 Words

12 Words

Think It-Feel It-Do It

Shirley Palmer

BROWN BOOKS
PUBLISHING GROUP

© 2015 Shirley Palmer

12 Words
Think It–Feel It–Do It

Brown Books Publishing Group
16250 Knoll Trail Drive, Suite 205
Dallas, Texas 75248
www.BrownBooks.com
(972) 381-0009

A New Era in Publishing™

ISBN 978-1-61254-246-1
Library of Congress Control Number 2015943336

Printed in the United States
10 9 8 7 6 5 4 3 2 1

For more information or to contact the author, please go to
www.ShirleyPalmer.com

I dedicate this book to my beloved parents, Thomas and Hester, and to my sister and best friend, Jackie. I love you.

Contents

Foreword
by Dr. James Rouse

Would you like to have a "blueprint" that served as a foundation to support you in building the life of your dreams? Would you be open to and could you be served well by having the architect of your most beautiful, meaningful, and abundant life blueprint be someone who knows all that goes into building your living masterpiece? And would it be inspiring and confidence building if you knew that the person who was "co-designing" with you was someone who has done all the necessary "groundwork" and continues to refine her craft of building and sustaining a living masterpiece? I know that I want all these things to support me in the creation of my most beautiful life, and I want these all for you, too.

I have had the blessing and honor of sharing a friendship and a true sister-and-brother-of-choice relationship with my dear, gifted, and beautiful teacher, mentor, and soul sister Shirley Palmer. Shirley has done her work personally, professionally, and, most importantly, spiritually. She is the perfect embodiment of power and grace, of courage and humility, of passion and compassion. In

12 Words, I found myself feeling at once passionate and empowered as well as peaceful and full of grace. Yes, Shirley's heart-centered teaching makes me feel possible.

If you are drawn to this book, I believe I know you. I trust that you are a seeker, a creative being, an artist, a warrior, a non-conformist, a goddess, a healer, a servant-leader, a disciple, and a believer in the power of your responsibility to become the person of your dreams. To be sure, this is why we are here. The twelve words will serve you well on your journey home. They will wake you up, they will nourish your heart and spirit, and they will bring you peace.

You can choose to read *12 Words* all at once like the most fulfilling twelve-course meal for your mind, body, and soul. Or you can read one "word" at a time, savoring its depth and enjoying its sweetness over and over again. My copy is now and forever set on my bedside table; *12 Words* serves me first thing in the morning to help me wake up to an intention, a vision, and a mission for how I wish to be living today. I also find my way home again each night by reading again a "word" to contemplate, under the influence of which to fall sleep peacefully.

Fortunately, you have found Shirley Palmer and her *12 Words* by divine appointment. This is your time to fall in love with your life, to become wildly and passionately awake to your highest and most beautiful expression of living. I am inspired by your quest to become the person of your dreams. I am grateful to my friend, my sister, and my soul teacher-mentor Shirley Palmer for serving us all with her wisdom, energy, and love. Let us take her offering of these twelve words and live each of them with our *hearts out loud*.

Love and blessings on your journey home,

Dr. James E. Rouse
Naturopathic doctor, speaker, entrepreneur,
and coauthor (along with Dr. Debra Rouse) of
Think Eat Move Thrive: The Practice for an Awesome Life

Introduction

> "Emotional Intelligence is a way of recognizing, understanding, and choosing how we think, feel, and act. It shapes our interactions with others and our understanding of ourselves. It defines how and what we learn; it allows us to set priorities; it determines the majority of our daily actions. Research suggests it is responsible for as much as 80% of the 'success' in our lives."
>
> Joshua Freedman

I am so very excited to bring *12 Words* to life with you and through you. This book brings together many helpful tools from the Think It—Feel It—Do It process that I use in my coaching and workshops. It presents twelve simple words that can show you how to play the game of life. The twelve words are: change, fear, courage, believe, trust, ask, intuition, action, purpose, happiness, love, and gratitude.

No doubt you are asking why these exact twelve words. Each word carries a power in its own right, but each also invokes thoughts, ideas, associations, and positive and negative emotions that can spur us to deeper levels of change in our lives. By briefly exploring each of these twelve simple but powerful words we can chart a course for rapid growth.

Think of *12 Words* as a "handbook for happiness." You can read it quickly and easily but also come back to it again and again, whenever you feel you are slipping off course.

Each chapter will take you on a three-part journey, Think It, Feel It, and Do It. In the *Think It* section you'll explore what the key word means to you. In the *Feel It* section, you'll have the chance to let the concept sink in emotionally through special exercises. And in the *Do It* section you'll incorporate each concept into *your* game of life through suggested practices and/or experiments. The work will be fun and playful, yet challenging, as I really want to help you learn, grow, succeed, and live your dream. I really wish someone had given me this book thirty years ago. I know I would have consumed it and would have been living my dream much sooner.

Let me tell you a little about me. I am no different from you. I have faced my share of challenges and crises. I have tried and failed at businesses and relationships that didn't suit me. But once I realized it was all a game, it became much easier to play.

I started life as a farmer's daughter in Northern Ireland. I didn't have the opportunity to go to university because my family couldn't afford it. The priority was for me to work and support myself and help my folks. Yet, in the back of my mind I had a vision of one day being my own boss, of being able to teach and help others.

Like most young people at the tender age of eighteen, I believed that life was about schooling, getting a job, marriage, starting a family, and hoping to earn a little extra so I could *enjoy* life, not just survive. My journey took me to London, where I worked hard, helped my family, and saved a little extra when possible. I failed in marriage and was terminated from jobs. At one point, I was searching for a job, studying a new career, and working in a restaurant just to pay my bills.

I went to work in the corporate world and spent eighteen years in an environment where I had to keep re-modeling myself to suit the business. Finally, I decided to go back to my dream and make it a reality. Today, I am proud to say I am my own boss. I teach and I help others master their lives. I am able to do this because I finally learned how to play the game.

How does the game work? Well, I can't give you all the answers here or you wouldn't read the book! But I will say this: it becomes easy when you learn the rules. Be heart-centered, open, and authentic. Be yourself, ask, share, care, use your intuition, ask for guidance, practice loving relationships, and always be grateful. Those are the keys.

Over the course of the book you will learn how to:

- Embrace change
- Put plans into action and become unstoppable
- Let go of fear, clear the blocks, and delete limiting beliefs
- Develop your self-confidence and self-belief
- Control your emotional mindset
- Maximize your potential
- Develop your courage and stop worrying

- Keep a positive attitude
- Communicate more positively
- Be more heart-centered
- Believe in yourself
- Learn how to trust your vibe
- Strengthen your relationships
- Ask and truly receive
- Change your money mindset
- Use your intuition daily
- Get into "the zone" via inspired action
- Find your life's purpose
- Acknowledge your values in life
- Be happy for no reason
- Love yourself, and love freely and deeply
- Live from a place of gratitude

The overall emphasis of the book will be to help you focus on your own emotional intelligence and use emotional information to guide your thinking and behavior.

I hope you enjoy the read and complete all the exercises. If you do, you will have a phenomenal toolkit with which to play your game of life. This toolkit will help you be more happy, joyful, successful, and grateful in all areas of your life.

Isn't it time for you to change your game?

With love,

Change

> *"Everyone thinks of changing the world, but no one thinks of changing himself."*
>
> Leo Tolstoy

Think It

What is change? As I see it, change is *chance*—the chance to learn and grow, to allow new opportunities to surface, to expand our horizons, and to move closer to our potential. As Tolstoy noted (above), we are always looking at how *others* should change—in our countries, our businesses, and our families—but in most cases the change has to start with ourselves.

The only real question is, Are *you* ready to change?

Change can run the gamut from tiny to huge. Change can be little more than a nuisance and can even happen unconsciously. On the other hand, it can be quite uncomfortable or excruciatingly painful. It can also be truly life-changing and transformational. Typically, the bigger and harder the change we face, the more growth potential it offers.

Change is happening all the time whether we choose to acknowledge it or even notice it. You are a different person than you were yesterday, or even a moment ago, simply by virtue of the thoughts, feelings, and actions you choose in this moment.

Many people ask me, "How long does it take to change?" The answer is that change happens the millisecond you accept it in your heart and mind. Once you truly accept that a change has happened or *will* happen, you immediately begin focusing on creating new habits—mental, emotional, physical, and even spiritual—to make the change a permanent one. You stop running *away* from the change and start running *toward* it.

When change happens around you, you need to ask yourself, "Can I respond to this change by changing myself?" You need to explore your own thoughts and feelings. How are they manifesting in reaction to this change? Which ones are positive and which ones are negative? Which ones will you hold onto or let go of? How will you choose to express your thoughts and feelings to deal with the changes around you? What thoughts, words, feelings, and actions might empower you to accept the change?

Can you see the potential opportunity hidden in the current change? Will you allow yourself to adapt to the change and to change your own life in response? Will you look beyond the pain and inconvenience to find something of value in the change and a potential takeaway that you can learn from?

If the change is too painful to deal with right now, can you allow yourself to just *be* with the change until you are ready to change? Sometimes changes are so unexpected, uncontrollable, and painful that all we can do is just be. That's OK. In those cases, we just need to stay with the pain and grief until it eventually lessens and we are able to get some perspective on the situation.

When big change happens, it is totally natural to have feelings of anger, sadness, frustration, or loss. It *is* beneficial, though, to talk to someone about these emotions or to write them down, as this will help you adapt to the change. Don't spend too much time *dwelling* in negative emotions. That will only keep you in a place of helplessness. You want to be in a place of newfound hope and growth. And change always offers that opportunity.

Don't beat yourself up because you are feeling scared or vulnerable. Vulnerability is just part of being human; it allows others to really see you as you are. It also helps you recognize where you might need help from others and allows you to accept that help. When you do feel the need to ask for help, empower yourself by being specific about the kind of help you need. Most importantly, remind yourself to seek and acknowledge your own inner guidance and to rely on its wisdom.

Going through a major life change like job upheaval, illness, divorce, or the loss of a loved one will change you forever—and that is a good thing. If you are willing to have perspective and vision, you will see that in the midst of change, there is immense learning and growth.

As change is taking place, you might find yourself asking the following questions:

- How am I supposed to grow from this?
- What am I supposed to learn?
- How will I become a better person because of this?

If you are open and receptive, the change *will* make you stronger and will enable a better version of you to emerge. Welcome this new you. Just because something changes about you, it doesn't change the core of who you are a person. You can remain grounded in your values and principles while you let go of habits and beliefs that are no longer serving you.

As you go through change, it is important to believe that things can and will get better and that you will see the light at the end of the tunnel. You must have faith that new and positive possibilities are emerging.

Change can present itself in two ways, either as a voluntary choice—such as a decision to become more fit or to learn new job skills—or as a shifting situation you are forced adapt to. Remember that humankind's ability to adapt is truly amazing. When you are presented with challenges, you will naturally find ways to solve your problems and change your behaviors, as long as you remain flexible and confident. If you think you cannot change and adapt, it is only because you have convinced yourself that this is the case. If you allow yourself to trust that you *can* adapt, then you will. And if you believe that you are capable of making positive, voluntary changes in your life, then you will, no matter what the challenge.

Life doesn't always give you the opportunity to prepare for a big change; you may sometimes find yourself overwhelmed by what is in front of you. In these circumstances, take baby steps, choosing one thing to work on at a time. Focus your attention on something manageable, and eventually you will be able to embrace the change and grow from it.

Learning to grow from change will help you move forward into the future rather than wallowing in your past. Each new day is an opportunity to begin again. Think about this: If you were totally open to change, where might you be, what might you be doing, and how might you be living a year from now? Five years from now? Why not consider what changes you are ready to make in your life and start today? What have you got to lose? Only old habits. What have you got to gain? Only everything.

> *"To exist is to change, to change is to mature, to mature is to go on creating oneself endlessly."*
>
> *Henri Bergson*

Feel It

Let's look at how you can bring about voluntary change that you *want* to make in your life. Write down the top three situations you feel you are struggling with in your life and that you want to change. This could be your current job, a relationship, or maybe a health issue, for example. Give each situation, as it stands right now, a mark of one to five, where five is excellent and one is poor. Now, for each of those three situations, write down some phrases to describe what it would look like if it was absolutely at its best. Let's use your job as an example. Describing your job at its best you might write, "I love it, it's in a great location, I am working with a fabulous team of people, I am paid an excellent salary, I just got promoted, I am currently working on some amazing projects."

Imagine all these conditions to be true *right now*. Allow yourself to feel the excitement of getting up each morning to go to work. Feel the blood rush through your veins at the anticipation of the day ahead. Imagine being inspired by the new projects you're working on and feeling the joy of the rewards that you are receiving in return for your input.

From that amazing future place, identify the baby steps of change that might be necessary for you to get there. What do they look like? What do they feel like? What key steps could you take right now to make a difference? Maybe you might consider some of these:

- Focus on the solutions rather than the problems.
- Let go of the negative voice in your head, and be more positive.
- Have an attitude of gratitude.
- Become more of a team player, and let the ego go.
- Research what is needed in your business.
- Learn new skills.
- Learn to become a heart-centered leader.

- Be flexible and adaptable.
- Ask for help and guidance.

Really try to see and feel the positive end results that can come from taking the baby steps needed.

Now go back to each of the three situations, and rescore yourself from one to five. How do you feel about each situation now? Perhaps you will see that the score has shifted upwards. Just the knowledge that you can start taking baby steps toward change often makes you feel more hopeful about a situation.

Of course, the above applies to situations where you have some measure of control, but what about when you don't have control? Sometimes change happens around you, and you just have to deal with it. Let's use the example of your job again. Imagine you have been terminated from your position involuntarily. How might you deal with that situation differently? That type of change will probably bring up feelings of fear and resistance.

Here are some ideas on how you can manage adaptive change:

- Understand that we do not necessarily resist change as much as we resist loss. Try to get in touch with your true feelings about whatever loss you believe you are suffering. Coming to a realistic understanding of your feelings about loss can greatly reduce the fear around change.
- Remember, *every* change has both pluses and minuses. Focus on the positives and the benefits.

Try to really *feel* what it will be like when these benefits take effect in your life.

- As the change is taking place, focus on the feeling of optimism, even if it only pops up for you in brief flashes. The more you focus on feelings of optimism instead of feelings of grief, disappointment, and anger, the more the feeling of optimism will grow.
- Examine your true feelings about your old situation (before the change took place). For example, were you truly happy in the old job? Was it paying you your worth? Did it really meet all your emotional needs? Weren't you, perhaps, ready for a new challenge on some level?

Do It

I love the Mary Engelbreit quote "If you don't like something, change it; if you can't change it, then change the way you think about it." This quote highlights the importance of the thought process as it relates to change.

Write down a few goals you may have for the coming year. Once you have decided which goals you will aim for, then you must (1) adopt the right mental approach, (2) create plans for achieving the goals, and (3) take action every single day to complete those plans. If you do these three things, you will become unstoppable.

With each goal I would encourage you to:

- Be specific. Don't be vague, using terms like "some" or "a little bit" or "more"—as in, for example, "I will earn *more* money" or "I will lose *some* weight." Put a concrete number in place.
- Keep it simple. Be clear and focused; don't over-complicate it.
- Make it measurable. You cannot achieve a pound of happiness or self-esteem, but you *can* get a new position that pays 20 percent more than your current job by December 1.
- Write the goal down, and look at it every single morning. This will help you focus on your priorities and objectives.
- Share your journey. If you know your team members, friends, and family support you in making the change, you'll be much more likely to stick to your plan and reach your goals. Find an "accountability buddy" if need be.
- Make sure your goal is aligned with your values. When your values and goals are in agreement, you will achieve your goals every single time.

Ask yourself what you can do today to start this process, what you can do tomorrow, what can you do next week, and so on. Embracing change instead of resisting it helps us grow into a grander version of ourselves, bringing us closer to living the life of our dreams.

To better adapt to unplanned change, you may also want to consider the following:

- Be aware that change happens and change is what keeps life fresh and interesting.
- Be attentive and conscious about what is happening around you at home and in the workplace. Notice where there are hints that change is on its way.
- Be flexible. Continually look for ways to improve your communications and your skill set. Always be open to seeking out new knowledge.
- Don't drown in uncertainty. Be willing to take bold steps and get actively involved in the process of change.
- Live for today and focus on the future; don't dwell in the past.

"Progress is impossible without change, and those who cannot change their minds cannot change anything."

George Bernard Shaw

Final Thoughts—Change

Change is a constant in our lives, and it is important to go with the flow instead of resisting it. This may mean adapting and remodeling ourselves, but this is how we learn and grow. Change may seem hard in the beginning and messy in the middle, but it is always gorgeous at the end.

My key thoughts are:

- Set small goals in order to make change manageable and enjoyable.
- Focus on solutions not problems.
- Let negativity and resistance go.
- Embrace change; don't avoid it or deny it.
- Learn and grow.
- Stay positive.
- Be flexible.
- Remember, you are always capable of changing your perspective.

Each change is a turning page. It is about closing one chapter and opening another one. By truly embracing change, you will begin to see amazing transformations in your life. These transformations can manifest as new routines, new opportunities, and a newfound sense of self-confidence.

Fear

> *"Build this day on a foundation of pleasant thoughts. Never fret at any imperfections that you fear may impede your progress."*
> *Og Mandino*

Think It

What is fear? Fear is a common emotion of dread or anxiety that often appears to be lurking in the shadows irrespective of whether the threat is real or imagined. I like to use the acronym False Evidence Appearing Real. So what I'm talking about here is mainly *false* fears, those imaginary ideas in our head that we dwell on, and the emotions we manifest in response to those ideas. Mental preconceptions we create about people and situations trigger a host of fears, including fear of the unknown, fear of failure, fear of being ridiculed, fear of disapproval, fear of inadequacy, even fear of "positive" things like success, love, and attention. Most of our fears are based on ideas in our heads, not on reality.

Here are some telltale signs that fear is creeping into your life and hijacking your mind:

- Self-doubt
- Negative self-talk
- Procrastination
- A knot in your stomach
- A sense of weight pressing down on your chest
- Inability to see things clearly
- Masking of your true emotions
- Frustration
- Loss of direction

Fear is the number one culprit responsible for holding millions of people back from growing as individuals, achieving success, and becoming the best version of themselves possible. The most successful people in life and in business tend to be those who learn to deal effectively with fear. But even the highest achievers sometimes get stymied by fear. They know that taking risks is a vital part in getting from where they are to where they want to go. But often these risks are met with fear, which can cause them to question their ambitions and prevent them from taking action.

How do you recognize fears, especially false ones, and overcome them? First you need to understand what the fear is and where it stems from. By identifying the root cause of the fear, you are in a stronger position to acknowledge it and deal with it. Often fears take root in us because we have accepted a belief in ourselves as weak or inadequate. This belief may have been "planted" in us by someone else. Perhaps a school teacher, a colleague, a parent, or a dear friend made a comment suggesting that you were not good enough, and though intellectually you might know it isn't true, you have decided to own that belief on an emotional level. This simple thought in the mind can play havoc with how you feel about yourself and create countless reasons for you to fear achievement and success.

So what can you do about it? By simply rewiring your brain, you can overcome your fears and develop the courage needed to get to where you want to go. Easier said than done, I know, but let's try. You might start by increasing your self-confidence through the use of daily mantras or affirmations or by reading uplifting books. For example, you may want to use affirmations like:

- I am good and strong enough.
- I trust my inner wisdom and intuition.
- I am safe and sound, and all is well.
- I love and approve of myself.

If, however, you deeply fear facing a certain goal or obstacle, then you need to allow yourself to acknowledge that fear. Allow yourself to walk with it and feel it. Ask your higher self for insight on why this fear is appearing in your life. Sometimes this is just as simple as asking the question "Why am I having this fear?" and being open enough to accept whatever you feel the answer to be.

Once you uncover the fear, real or imagined, it is imperative to take action. Without action, you cannot overcome it. The fear will put down roots and, if you allow it, can last a lifetime. So do something to counter it. It is OK to take baby steps just as long as you are moving forward in a positive direction.

Let's look at an example. Suppose you are unhappy in your job but you are not quite ready to move on because you are afraid you won't be able to find and keep another job. Baby steps you could take might include researching the job market to check what is available, updating your CV, improving your profile on the various professional social media networks, and/or signing up for a training course to bolster your marketable skills.

Each step is a move forward, and you have nothing to lose. You can always ask yourself what the worst-case scenario is—"If I do this what would the worst possible outcome be?" This will help you clarify your thoughts and fears and help you assess what you are capable of dealing with.

In early childhood, we didn't live with fear. When we were learning to walk, we didn't worry about embarrassment or failure. We fell down over and over again until we got better at staying on our feet. We played, had fun, and thought we were supermen or superwomen. Can you imagine if you could do anything in the world without feeling fear or any negative feelings whatsoever? You would be unstoppable.

Well, you *can* learn to be childlike again by developing a new relationship with "failure."

Let's face it; failure is inevitable at some stage in your life, and sooner or later you will have to overcome your fear of it. Instead of fearing failure, see it as a blessing in disguise. After all, it is not through success that we become wise but through our failures. Allow yourself to take action, knowing that if failure is the outcome, it will point you to the next step you need to take. If you take this attitude, you can learn to embrace failure rather than fear it.

Another great way to overcome fear is to learn to live in the present moment. Most of us live in our past or our future. We spend much of our time regretting what we've done before or worrying about what is to come. The secret is to learn from the past, stay with the present, and not let your mind run uncontrollably into the future, creating fears about what *might* happen. Stay in the now. There is no room for fear in the now.

Some simple ways to get out of your head include going for a walk and getting some fresh air, playing a musical instrument, or going for a run. If a fear is persistent and intrusive, write it down. Consider discussing it with a friend, colleague, coach, or other professional who can help you. The process of describing your fear can help you get it out of your head and understand what it is about and whether it is real or imaginary. The key is to recognize your thoughts for what they are—just thoughts.

> *"Nothing in life is to be feared. It is only to be understood."*
>
> Marie Curie

Feel It

Let's focus on a great exercise that will help you allow freedom into your life and release the fear and negative emotions. Remember, you are not your emotions, and although emotions are useful, they also sometimes hold us back.

Let's get started:

- Lower your head, and place your hand on your chest or your stomach.
- Get in touch with a particular fear (and/or negative emotion) that is troubling or challenging you right now. This could also be a current situation that has a strong negative emotional charge for you.
- Notice the intensity of the feeling in your body, and rate it from 0 to 10, with 10 being the most intense.
- Welcome the emotion much as you would welcome a friend into your home. You don't need to eagerly endorse the emotion; just embrace it, accept it, welcome it. Allow it to be there instead of pretending it doesn't exist. Feel it completely without judging it. Feel it in your body as well as in your heart and mind.

- Repeat the process. How does it feel this time? Rate the intensity again, from 0 to 10. Maybe now it's a 7, 5, or 3?
- Repeat again.
- Ideally you want to come to zero and recognize that the fear/emotion no longer has any charge over you whatsoever. But if your number is 3 or lower, that is OK, too. Try it again later, and see if you can get it to zero.

Letting go of the emotional charge associated with the fear is a great way to open up the clogged plumbing in your energy system and move forward in your life.

Do It

Really getting clear on what is scaring you can instantly diffuse the anxiety bomb ticking in your mind. I'd like to share the "Why" exercise in order to show you just how simple this is.

Start by thinking of three fears that you feel are blocking you right now. Then go through the following process, which will help you see the reasons behind your fears:

- Write the three fears down. Take your time with this, and be honest.
- Pick one of the three fears, and focus on it.
- Got it in your head?
- Now ask yourself, "Why am I afraid of X?"

- Answer it.
- Ask again.
- Why?
- Answer again. (You can give the same answer, but eventually you'll need to get unstuck and move on to a different reply.)
- Keep repeating the *Why* question, and keep answering it.

Through the process of basic repetition, you can drill down and find the true source of your fear. The exercise is even more powerful if you do it with a person you fully trust.

Here is an example of someone who was afraid of getting sacked, or laid off:

Q. What are you afraid of?
A. I'm afraid of getting sacked.

Q. Why are you afraid of getting sacked?
A. Because I make great money and don't want to lose my salary.

Q. Why are you afraid of getting sacked?
A. Because competition is tough in my sector.

Q. Why are you afraid of getting sacked?
A. Because I will be humiliated.

Q. Why are you afraid of getting sacked?
A. Because I will have to tell my mother.

Q. Why are you afraid of getting sacked?

A. Because then my mother would have another reason to think I am never going to amount to anything.

Q. Why are you afraid of getting sacked?

A. Because I'll never get the love I want from my mother.

Ah. Now we've arrived at the real source of the fear. This person is afraid of losing the love of his/her mother.

Quite often the fear will ease considerably once you fully appreciate where it stems from. If not, allow yourself to see the fear as a traveling companion but not a driver. Let it be there, but don't give it power. Let it sit in the passenger seat, but don't take direction from it or stop moving forward because of it.

> *"We gain strength, and courage, and confidence by each experience in which we really stop to look fear in the face . . . we must do that which we think we cannot."*
>
> *Eleanor Roosevelt*

Final Thoughts—Fear

When we are afraid, we pull back from life. However, by allowing ourselves to recognize the fear for what it is and not letting it control us, we can move forward. Do one thing every day that scares you. In that way, you can make fear a positive motivator in your life. Step out of your comfort zone, and work on becoming comfortable with the uncomfortable. This will help you remove the barriers that were once holding you back. It will also translate into increased confidence and maximize your freedom.

My key thoughts are:

- Be fully present with your fear, and ask, "Is it true?"
- Ask, "What is the worst that can happen?"
- Pay attention to your thoughts and emotions.
- Rewire your brain via mantras, affirmations, inspirational reading, etc.
- Do one thing every day that scares you.
- Fear is False Evidence Appearing Real.
- Talk about your fear, and release it.

3

Courage

> *"Courage is about doing what you're afraid to do. There can be no courage unless you're scared. Have the courage to act instead of react."*
>
> *Oliver Wendell Holmes*

Think It

What is courage? Courage is the quality of mind or spirit that enables a person to face difficulty, danger, and pain in spite of the fear that may be present. It comes from the French word *coeur*, which means "heart." I like to think of courage as an emotional muscle—the more you practice it, the stronger it becomes.

I believe we must step into courage daily if we wish to live a life beyond our expectations and dreams. Many ordinary people somehow find the courage to overcome both physical and psychological barriers to accomplish great goals and solve enormous problems in their lives.

Courage is not the absence of fear. Courage is acknowledging the fear and doing the thing nevertheless. People often think that courage has to be big, like base jumping or giving a talk to a thousand people. It doesn't. Courage is whatever is required to push you out of your comfort zone. I would urge you to take baby steps to build the courage you need in your life today. Start small, but start somewhere. As you take small steps of courage, you will build up the "muscle" to take greater ones.

An act of courage could be:

- Trying a new activity without letting your self-image interfere
- Starting a blog
- Joining Toastmasters
- Worrying less, acting more
- Listening more, talking less
- Starting a book club
- Stopping smoking
- Asking your boss for a raise
- Waking up at 5:00 a.m. and writing for an hour or two before work
- Admitting when you are wrong
- Picking one incomplete thing in your life (an article you want to write, a cluttered home you want to clean, a craft you want to learn) and doing it for fifteen minutes every day

A large part of developing courage is having faith in yourself, faith in a higher power, and faith that things will work out. You can gain this type of confidence by keeping a positive mindset and allowing yourself to visualize a favorable outcome. By developing your courage, you will empower yourself to face your problems head on, as well as to acquire the skills needed to deal with life's inevitable obstacles and challenges.

Let me share with you one of my brave moments. Believe me; at first I didn't think it was courageous; in fact, I thought it might very well be extremely stupid. I was working in the private equity sector, had a good job, and was well paid, but there was something missing in my life. It was taking its toll on me mentally, physically, and spiritually. I no longer loved my work, and I wasn't growing. I finally decided it was time to pluck up the courage to quit my job. Like most people, I was rooted to the floor by fear and had trouble escaping from the steel shackles of the job I was in. Once I gave my notice, though, the weight lifted from my shoulders, my mind became calmer and more at ease, and I felt I could move forward positively again. That led to the beginning of my first business, which was the start of a new journey toward fulfilling my dream.

It takes courage each day to be open to new possibilities, to fuel our dreams, and to inspire and help others. Maybe it is time for you to ask yourself what you need to do courageously today. Here are some possible areas where you might need to be more courageous in your life:

- Learn to communicate openly and frequently.
- Learn to listen more and ask for honest feedback instead of automatically defending yourself.
- Be more accountable for your own actions, and stop passing the buck.

- Pay attention to your body, and take the steps necessary to improve your health.
- Ask for guidance with something that's causing you difficulty at work.
- Share an honest, constructive criticism with someone.
- Ask someone to go on a social outing with you.
- Stop the worrying—it serves no purpose—and face the problem head on.
- Think *thrive* rather than just *survive*.

Lastly, I would ask you to consider having courage to stand up for others and to make sure that every person in your world is being treated as a human being regardless of race, color, religion, ethnicity, or sexual preference.

I see courage every day in the struggles of average people striving to live well. I see it in my clients who have chosen to face their fears, better their lives, and live their dreams. I see it in the actions of leaders who have decided to do what they feel is right, not just what's expedient.

I would ask you to commit to being brave and gutsy today and to honor the bravery of others. Be one of those rare individuals who inspires families, children, colleagues, and friends by living from a place of courage.

"Courage doesn't always roar. Sometimes courage is the quiet voice at the end of the day saying, 'I will try again tomorrow.'"
Mary Anne Radmacher

Feel It

Grab a pen and a notebook, and find yourself a quiet space where you know you will not be interrupted. Let's begin this next exercise with the statement "Feel the fear and do it anyway." Write it down, and sit with it for a moment. Then allow yourself to openly and truthfully answer the following questions.

First, think about a situation in your childhood where you faced your fear even though you felt afraid.

- What did you and/or the people around you think, say, or do to help you face the fear?
- At what point did the fear start to dissipate?
- How did you feel afterwards?

Second, think about a situation in your adult life where you faced your fear even though you felt afraid. Now apply the same three questions. How did it feel this time? Did the feeling differ from that of the childhood memory?

Now think of a current situation you are facing that creates anxiety or fear. What is it that you are most afraid of?

Try to look at your current situation with a fresh pair of eyes. Picture yourself as having the skill set necessary to deal with the fear or anxiety. Allow yourself, in your mind, to be courageous by reminding yourself of how you pushed through and overcame those previous fears as a child and then as an adult.

Lastly, put the pen and pad down, and follow this guidance.

- Sit in a comfortable position, keeping your arms and legs uncrossed.
- Close your eyes, and release all thoughts of fear and anxiety.
- Imagine you are breathing in positivity and love. Picture light flooding through your body as you inhale.
- As you breathe out, release all the negativity.
- Repeat this several times.
- Breathe deeply again, and allow your mind to clear.
- Allow yourself to paint the picture in your mind's eye of having been courageous and pushing through the problem or issue. Imagine you are now seeing the positive results.
- Feel how wonderful this feels, and notice how there was no need to be worried.
- Allow yourself to *feel* the power of having courage. Let the feeling permeate your body. Sit in this wonderful energy for several minutes.

Then grab your pen and notebook again, and remind yourself how wonderful it felt to embrace courage. Describe the feeling on paper as best you can. Add as much physical detail as possible, and don't forget the emotions.

If perchance you are dealing with something incredibly difficult in your life right now, I would suggest that you repeat this exercise for seven days and then acknowledge how courageous you have been in facing the fear and acting on it.

Do It

Do you remember the last time you took a leap of faith? Was it in a relationship? Was it at your job? Was it at home? Was it on an adventure? Here is a simple step-by-step exercise to help you summon the courage you need today:

- Relax your mind, and look back on your life.
- Comb through your past, and search for benefits you would not be enjoying today if you had not acted with tremendous courage. Perhaps, for example, you asked someone to dance, and now you are married to that person and have two beautiful children. Maybe you asked your boss for more responsibility, and now you are the head of your department.
- Remind yourself how you conquered your fear, became more self-aware, found your strengths, and faced the adversity in front of you.
- Now focus on your future, and think of three major goals that you want to achieve.

- Try to identify the fears associated with achieving these desired accomplishments, the fears that are holding you back and that require peak courage on your part to overcome.
- Now think of one action—the most courageous one—that you can take *today* toward accomplishing each of these goals.
- Now . . . put that action in motion. Take a step. Do something.

Courage is not a one-time thing; it must be practiced time and time again throughout your life. So make it a lifelong positive habit! It gets easier the more you do it.

> *"You must be courageous and brave, and not fearful, in taking advantage of life's opportunities as they are made available to you."*
>
> *Alberto Posse*

Final Thoughts—Courage

They say it takes a village to accomplish anything worthwhile, but often that village is spurred into action by the courage of one person. Be courageous in your life today, and take on your boldest dream. Develop your emotional muscle of courage with small baby steps. Keep trying new things, and have a positive attitude while facing any problems you may have to deal with. Think *thrive* rather than *survive*. Inspire others with your courage.

My key thoughts are:

- Exercise the muscle of courage every day.
- Courage is feeling the fear and doing it anyway.
- Start small, but start somewhere—build your courage like a muscle.
- Have faith in yourself, and know that things will work out.
- Keep a positive mindset and attitude.
- Communicate openly and frequently, asking for feedback and guidance.
- Have the courage to stand up for what is right.

Believe

"If you believe you can, you probably can. If you believe you won't, you most assuredly won't. Belief is the ignition switch that gets you off the launching pad."

Denis Waitley

Think It

Belief means many things to many people. So let's talk about a very specific type of belief—namely, self-belief. To have self-belief means to have confidence in oneself and one's abilities without being held back by doubt. It also means trusting in one's positive characteristics and self-worth. I am certain that having self-belief is a major key to successfully and happily playing the game of life.

How many things have you avoided doing or trying simply because you lacked self-belief?

The mind creates self-doubt. It questions your abilities, and you find yourself saying, "Can I really do this?" Or maybe it convinces you that other people are better, smarter, more worthy than you, or that you can't afford to risk failure. Or that success is for others but not the likes of you!

I believe that every human being truly wants success and the best that life can offer. Success means many positive things, but it also means freedom from worries, fears, and doubts. To develop self-belief and make successful changes in your life, it is important to empower the mind with positive suggestions and visualizations. First of all, you have to understand your negative beliefs in order to develop more positive ones. You are in complete control of the beliefs and pictures that you put in your head, but you may have forgotten this fact. All of your behaviors and choices are based on the image of yourself that you hold in your mind. Therefore, by changing that image for the better, your life will improve as well.

Belief is changed, for the better or worse, not by intellect alone but by changing the pictures in your brain. This goes for any aspect of your life. Whether you want success, wealth, a new home, a promotion, to run a marathon, to climb the mountain, to be a great husband or wife, or to become an entrepreneur, you must first picture yourself already having achieved it.

Sometimes that requires making immediate changes in your life or your environment. For example, let's imagine you don't like your job. It will be extremely difficult for you to have the positive mental picture necessary for success and achievement within your company. How can you visualize success in a place you don't like? Answer: you can't! Self-belief comes not just from trying to convince yourself you can do things. True self-belief comes from developing a powerful vision that you can be a great mother or father, a successful entrepreneur, an accomplished singer or author, or whatever it is you wish to believe you can do or be. You must *support* that vision with the choices you make in the here and now. If you want to be a great writer, you must start writing every day. If you want to be successful in your career, you must pick a career you love. If your present conditions and behaviors run counter to your vision, that vision will never get traction.

It is important to recognize that having self-belief doesn't mean that you are perfect or that you become arrogant. Rather, it means that you know and understand your weaknesses. You grant yourself the freedom to make mistakes and don't judge yourself because of them.

Imagine who you would be if you didn't have that little voice in your head telling you that you are not good enough, clever enough, or capable enough. Imagine if you could stop finding excuses *not* to set the goals or dream the dreams, and instead just went after your desires, full-steam ahead.

Give yourself permission to see *you* as a first-class person. Stop underestimating yourself! Before long, you will see that good things start to happen. Here are some additional thoughts to consider:

- If you are competing with someone else, think, *I am equal to the best.*
- When opportunities arise, think, *I can do it.*

- Master the thought *I believe in me, and I will succeed*.
- Pay attention to your self-talk—keep it loving and positive.
- Remind yourself daily how good you are.
- Believe big.

Successful people are just ordinary people who have developed belief in themselves and what they do. Remember, if you think little goals and expect little achievements, what will you achieve? Think big and win big.

> *"When you believe 'I can do it,' the 'how to do it' develops."*
>
> *David Schwartz*

Feel It

By getting into the habit of sitting down, closing your eyes, and visualizing yourself behaving decisively, calmly, and strongly, you can learn from yourself how to be confident, have self-belief, and behave in ways that maximize your chance of success. Watching videos of others who have been successful can also be helpful.

Let's try this exercise. Sit comfortably, and close your eyes.

- Try imagining you are viewing yourself on a TV screen.

- Place the on-screen version of you in a setting that reflects your highest hopes and dreams. For example, if you want to be a top screenwriter, you might picture yourself in a major film studio, doing a table reading of your latest script with some of the most famous actors in the movie business. "On-screen you" is showing "watching you" how to act with total self-belief.
- Picture the scene in its entirety. Really see where you are and who is around you.
- Feel the joy and happiness in your body as you watch yourself behave with confidence, assuredness, and grace.
- Feel the excitement at achieving your goals and success. Notice where you are feeling that excitement in your body.
- Take in the compliments from others—well done, congratulations, great job. But allow yourself to be heart-centered, not ego-driven.
- Notice how you hold your body with strength and confidence. Hear the firm, unapologetic tone of your voice.
- Take note of how success in your field has enhanced your life.
- Feel how your self-belief becomes stronger and stronger as you watch yourself behave confidently on screen.

The more you do this, the more you'll find that you will very naturally start to become like the **you** in the movie.

One of my dreams was to have my own radio show. So I first allowed myself to sit with the thought of having my own show. I thought about what I would call it, what topics I would cover, how long it would run for, and where I would find my audience. I imagined how I would feel when I was on my show.

Then I pictured myself on a TV screen actually doing the show, as I've encouraged you to do. In essence, I allowed myself to believe that I could do it by repeatedly playing the image in my mind and taking some action.

I had my own radio show in no time at all.

Do It

A great way to begin practicing self-belief in the real world is to think about the language you use when talking about yourself or your ideas. Your language can be disempowering or it can be what I call "transformational vocabulary." The latter involves using strong, positive, affirmative, non-apologetic words and expressions. Why "transformational"? Because the simple act of using this powerful language helps transform you into the confident person you want to be.

- Do you say "just" a lot, for example, as in "I am just concerned that . . ." Notice how the word "just" minimizes the validity or impact of what you have to say.

- Do you often say, "Sorry but . . ." Are you always offering an apology for your observations and opinions?

- Is "Does that make sense?" one of your favorite expressions? Do you see how this immediately tells your listener that you don't think you communicated your idea well?

- Do you say, "actually . . ." a lot? For example, "I actually disagree"? Notice how this makes it sound as if you are surprised by your own opinion and are making a slight apology for it.

- Do you often use expressions like "I guess," "this is probably irrelevant, but . . .," "not that I'm an expert," or filler sounds such as "um," "like," and "ah"? Do these reflect confidence and self-belief?

- Try to use transformational vocabulary instead.

- Drop the "just." Instead of saying, "I am just concerned that . . ." say, "I am concerned that . . ."

- Ask yourself if there is really any need for an apology.

- Instead of saying, "Does that make sense?" ask, "What are your thoughts on that?"

- Leave out the "actually" and own your reactions and opinions.

- Always speak kindly of yourself and others.

*"Others believing in you is nice but worthless
if not matched by your own thought."*
Scott Moore

Final Thoughts—Believe

Until we truly believe in ourselves, no one else will. Try to identify and clear the blocks that are holding you back from fully believing in yourself. Create your own movie, called your life, in which you have the starring role. Always use positive and transformative language when you are talking about yourself. Allow yourself to imagine, believe in, and create your magical world.

My key thoughts are:

- Self-belief can be learned.
- Whatever the mind can conceive and believe, it can achieve.
- Fake it until you make it.
- Create a great vision of yourself.
- Make choices today that support your vision for the future.
- Start small but think big.
- Practice transformational vocabulary.

5

Trust

"Trust is the glue of life. It's the most essential ingredient in effective communication. It's the foundational principle that holds all relationships."

Stephen Covey

Think It

What is trust? Trust is the belief that someone or something is reliable, good, honest, effective, and worthy of our faith and confidence. However, the key to all trust lies in trusting ourselves.

Trust encompasses nearly every aspect of our daily lives. Presence or absence of trust sets the tone of our relationships with ourselves and with others, including family, friends, coworkers, and even our country. I believe we are hard-wired to trust each other provided we are brought up in a safe, nurturing, and caring environment. Sadly, in today's society, many people are not so fortunate. Others, through disappointing life experiences, have learned to lower their "set point" of trust in their lives. However, trust *can* be relearned and re-earned.

As children we are all sensitive beings, totally receptive and open to trusting everything and everyone. Over time, our egos and minds take over. Toss in some experiences where we feel betrayed, sprinkle in a little imagination, and somewhere along the path our trust gets ruptured. Once it is ruptured, it becomes fragile and, like an eggshell, can be completely shattered with the next bad experience. When that happens, we lapse into "self-protective" mode. It's true that if you avoid people and don't let them get too close, you greatly reduce the risk of being hurt. But this could also greatly reduce your level of trust. Trust is essential for a happy life.

As Stephen Covey says, "Trust is the glue of life." It bonds us to each other and strengthens our relationships. It takes two to trust, though, and it is important to remember that if one person seeks only to be trusted but never to trust, the other will eventually stop taking all the risks and shut down the relationship.

To relearn and re-earn trust, you must start with yourself. Here are some thoughts on how to do it:

- Be truthful. To everyone. All the time. No excuses allowed for the small white lie. Your word must be your bond. If you can't speak truthfully about something, don't speak at all.
- Build your self-confidence. Learn to rely on yourself above all others. Take time to acknowledge your abilities, talents, positive traits, and values.

- Make and keep promises to yourself. Don't tell another living soul about these promises; they are between you and the universe. Nothing builds self-trust faster than making and keeping private promises. If you can't trust yourself, after all, who can you trust?

- Make and keep promises to others. Become comfortable with giving your word and following through. All promises carry equal weight; it doesn't matter whether they are big or small.

- Be a person of character and values. By acting with integrity, you will invite reliable, principled, and truthful people into your inner circle. Like attracts like.

- Communicate openly. If you have an issue with someone, get that issue out in the open and talk about it until it is resolved. Don't carry hidden resentments and bottled-up anger. Don't "act out" in passive-aggressive ways.

- Apologize where necessary. Own up to your errors, rather than lie or try to place the blame elsewhere.

- Show people that you care about them and are willing to trust them, even if they have let you down before. Trust them, and they in turn will trust you.

- Take risks. We like to think if we don't take risks, we won't fail. But the truth is the exact opposite of that: we fail by *not* taking risks. You won't know that you can trust yourself unless you take a risk and prove it.

- Compile a list of all the current ways you trust yourself. You may find that your level of self-trust varies in different areas of your life. You might trust yourself as a professional, for example, but not as a parent or love partner. Pick an area where your self-trust is low; make, *and keep* a promise to yourself in that area.

- Set healthy boundaries. Don't say yes when you mean no or vice-versa. Don't allow yourself to be manipulated.

- Honor and respect your own feelings. If you want to learn to trust yourself, it is essential that you trust your own feelings, especially those intuitive feelings that can give you guidance on your decision-making process.

Do you see how all trust flows from self-trust? Do you see that you can build your self-trust through your own actions and attitudes?

By trusting ourselves, we develop confidence in our own ability to take care of ourselves. In this way, we become less reliant on other people, which gives us the ability to look at others more objectively and truthfully, and with less neediness. This means if we are in a friendship, love relationship, or business partnership, we can start to see the other person for who they really are, without superimposing past situations on them or denying problematic behavior on their part.

By communicating more truthfully with ourselves, we can move confidently towards improving our communication with others, which is the foundation of trust.

> *"Self-trust is the first secret of success."*
> *Ralph Waldo Emerson*

Feel It

A great way to help you build trust, especially with yourself, is to learn to trust your "vibe." By "vibe" I mean that beneficial sixth sense that allows you to partner up with your higher self and receive useful guidance on how to live your life. As with any partnership, the trust and confidence will develop naturally through practice.

One of the simplest ways to build trust in your vibe is to carry a notebook or smart phone and jot a quick note to yourself every time you get a gut feeling, a "sixth" sense, or a vibe about anything. Make sure you don't let your ego take over by analyzing or judging it. Just notice the feelings and how they present themselves in your body.

Your vibe can be as simple as having an instinct to get some rest rather than spend the evening trying to finish a project, or intuiting that you are going to receive some good news when the phone rings. Don't worry if these vibes appear silly or irrelevant, or if you think you are simply imagining them—write them down anyway. Over time you will see that every vibe you have makes sense in one way or another.

Once a week, you might want to read over your vibes list. I am confident that you will see evidence as to why your gut feeling presented itself and will begin to learn for yourself the importance of trusting your own sixth sense.

I encourage my clients to do this for a minimum of three weeks. I watch in amazement every time as their confidence grows as a result of collecting solid evidence that their vibe is worth trusting. Before long, you will be allowing yourself to fully trust your sixth sense, and it will become a way of life for you.

Do It

Here are some additional thoughts on how you can reclaim your trust and begin putting it into action in your daily life.

Set the Intention

What if something greater than us is responding to our needs and desires and guiding us? Doesn't it make sense to set the daily intention to trust in this "something"? By setting this intention of trust, you are lowering your anxiety level and allowing yourself to be fully open to the benefits that will soon be coming your way.

You might want to consider writing a "what I trust" list that covers all aspects of your life. For example:

- I trust that the money will come.
- I trust that I can rely on my friends.

- I trust that the project will succeed.
- I trust that new clients will come.
- I trust that my guides are watching over me.

Tune In to Nature

I believe nature is our best teacher when it comes to trust. The sun rises and sets, the moon and stars emerge each night, the tide ebbs and flows, the grass grows, and the seasons change. All of this simply *is*. We trust that Mother Nature will handle all the details. By allowing yourself to tune in to nature, you come back to your natural sense, regain your balance, and recognize the role you play as a part of the jigsaw puzzle of this universe. Deep down, we all know that nature is in balance and flow and that we are an integral part of it. We can learn to trust in nature's cyclical energy in our own lives—suffering gives way to joy, problems give way to solutions.

Meditate

Allow yourself to connect with your higher self by sitting in silence or with some soft meditative music, trusting your inner wisdom to guide you on your path. Or try imagining yourself lying on a beautiful sandy beach, hearing the ocean, feeling the warmth of the sun, and knowing that by sinking into the warm sand, you are trusting yourself more and more. Feel the vulnerability of that trust, and know that it is through being vulnerable that we gain our true strength (which comes from a source far greater than our individual ego).

*"As soon as you trust yourself, you will know
how to live."*

Johann Wolfgang von Goethe

Final Thoughts—Trust

Trust is fundamental to any relationship, business or personal, but we must learn to trust ourselves first. This can be one of the most challenging tasks in our lives, but one that is well worth the effort. For only after gaining self-trust will others trust us. Build up your self-confidence, take risks, and allow yourself to hard-wire the trust of childhood back into your life. Ensure that you set good boundaries, and honor your thoughts and feelings, too.

My key thoughts are:

- Build your self-confidence.
- It is never too late to relearn and re-earn trust.
- Trust is the cornerstone of all your relationships.
- Keep all promises, big and small.
- Set your daily intention to trust and be trusted.
- Connect with nature and its trustworthy rhythms.
- Create a trust list.
- Always trust your vibe.

6

Ask

> "Asking is the beginning of receiving. Make sure you don't go to the ocean with a teaspoon. At least take a bucket so the kids won't laugh at you."
>
> *Jim Rohn*

Think It

Why is it that so many of us cringe at the thought of asking someone for a favor or simply asking for help? Why are we reluctant to even ask questions of *ourselves*? Let's face it; if we don't ask, the answer will always be no.

Some people might feel that asking makes them look needy and vulnerable. Others may feel that asking is tantamount to begging, which they see as beneath them. Still others may be reluctant to inconvenience the other person with their request. For many of us, though, our hesitancy comes from the simple fear of rejection and of hearing the answer no. Even asking a question of ourselves can be intimidating. We may be afraid of the answer we're going to get, or maybe that we won't get an answer at all.

When you need help, do you ask for it? Or do you just get a tad frustrated, feeling helpless and hoping to be "rescued"? When was the last time you asked for guidance or help? Did you ask your partner/husband/wife? Was it a friend? When was the last time you *wanted* to ask something—for a raise, for an introduction, or even for an upgrade when renting a car—but didn't? Do you have an "ask" on your mind today? If so, what is it?

What if the answer to your question is yes not no?

Practicing non-attachment when you ask for something is a great way to become more comfortable with asking. Do not be attached to getting a yes or no answer. By simply letting go of the outcome even as you ask the question, you can remove all of the anxiety over "What if the answer is no?" If the answer *is* no, perhaps you can come back and ask again at a better time. (Of course, there may be occasions when asking twice really isn't advisable. For example, asking the same person for the same favor a second time might be deemed as forceful and selfish. Be fully aware of why the "no" was there in the first instance.)

To rid yourself of the feeling that asking for a favor creates indebtedness, get in the habit of offering to do a favor in return for every favor asked. A simple "How can I thank you?" is a beautiful show of gratitude and exchange. But remember this, too: most people get a good feeling from helping others. Perhaps they remember a time when they were in a similar position and are glad for an opportunity to balance the scales. Life is a 50/50 blend of give and take. You must be as willing to receive as you are to give. If you habitually have trouble accepting gifts and favors from others, you hamper *their* ability to be generous and giving. That's just as bad as being a constant taker.

It is important to be specific but also flexible in your asking. This will make it easier for both you and the person you are asking. If you appear indecisive and unsure of what you want, your request will come off as weak and the other person will not know how to respond. Show the person how much you really want the favor, but also be polite and show flexibility. Remember, you're not making a demand, you're making a request.

As difficult as it may be to ask of others, it can be even harder to ask things of ourselves. Asking deep and reflective questions about what we truly want is terrifying to many of us. But as Leo Babauta says, "At the end of the day, the questions we ask of ourselves determine the type of people that we will become." Most of us want the same *basic* things in life, irrespective of ethnic backgrounds or culture. We tend to want validation, love, happiness, fulfillment, prosperity, good health, and a better future. It's easy to answer questions about these basic things. Think about it. If I were to ask you what you wanted most out of life, in one quick sentence, what would your answer be? It might be something like "I want to be happy and have a healthy family and a well-paid job." But these superficial "basic needs" questions generally keep us stuck. I would encourage you instead to ask questions that will really help you move forward in life. Here are some examples of deeper questions to consider:

- What old rejections are still holding me back today?
- How is my ego getting in the way of my desires?
- If we learn from our mistakes, why am I always so afraid to make a mistake?
- Based on my current daily routines and actions, where can I see myself in five years?
- What do I need to spend more or less time doing?
- What impact do I want to have on the world?
- What am I procrastinating about at this present moment?
- If I haven't achieved it yet, what do I have to lose by trying?
- What can I do in the next week that will bring more joy, passion, and purpose to my life?

Exploring these questions will help you to determine what is important to you and see where you are getting in your own way. By asking relentlessly honest questions of yourself, you will find it easier to ask honest questions of others. And by being willing to help yourself, you will be more open to asking for help from others.

> "The strong individual is the one who asks for help when he needs it."
> *Rona Barrett*

Feel It

If you want to discover more about yourself and the asking process, here is a perfect exercise to undertake. Choose up to seven people from various avenues of your life—friends, family members, coworkers, people you know from social and community activities. Start each day by asking one person a few simple but revealing questions about you, for example:

- 🖋 What are my best talents?
- 🖋 What are my strengths and weaknesses?
- 🖋 What do you love most about me?
- 🖋 What do you find irritating or unlikeable about me?

Encourage totally honest answers, and be thankful for the answers you receive. Once you compile all the answers at the end of the week, you will clearly see what others think and feel about you. Notice your own feelings as you compare their answers to your own self-perceptions. Are you surprised? Disappointed? Angered? Touched? Why?

Another "ask" you might want to consider is one to your higher self and/or to the universe itself. Assuming you want more money in your life (who doesn't?), this can be quite a fun and playful exercise. I call it the penny game. Over the next three days, ask the universe to send you pennies, and set an inner intention to spot them. They can be in your car, in your pocket, on the ground, absolutely anywhere.

Focus on the *feeling* of how exciting it is to find a penny (positive mindset) not "Why aren't there any pennies around?" (negative mindset). The key is to privately celebrate each time you find one. Feel real joy. Imagine you have just won the lottery. Get really silly with it. Dance, sing, and remember to thank your higher self and the universe for the gift of the penny. I guarantee one thing: you'll find a lot of them.

By simply celebrating "pennies from heaven," you will have cleared some of your abundance blockages and gained some new beliefs, such as "Money is easy to come by." The universe, for its part, does not recognize that it is only a penny and will continue to deliver more and more money to you, in larger denominations.

Do It

Let's imagine life is presenting you challenges that are causing you pain, anguish, and/or stress, and you are ready to ask for help. How can you gain the best help and advice to overcome these challenges? Here are some suggestions:

1. Ask the right person for help. You want to ensure that you will be listened to and understood and that the person you ask will be someone who is compassionate about your situation but also experienced enough to give you the correct guidance.

2.   Ask clearly. In order to do this, you must first be clear on what you want. Get a mental picture in your mind. A fun and easy way to do this is to create a mini-movie in your imagination of exactly what you are asking for. Let yourself really see it and feel it, and add in as much detail as you can. Keep it positive.

3.   Be specific. Let's use the example of asking for a pay raise. If you want to see more money in your paycheck each week or month, ask yourself how much. What would it feel like to have a 5 percent increase? What about 10 percent? Which one feels better? Using the mini-movie exercise above, allow yourself to play out the scene with your boss. See the money in your bank account and on your weekly or monthly pay slip, and imagine you have been given the 10 percent raise. The result? You will be no worse off for asking, but ideally you will have gotten what you asked for. Even if you don't get it immediately, you have put your desire on the table and now your boss is aware that you would like a raise. That may result in your getting your next raise sooner than if you had kept your mouth shut.

Each of these three steps can be applied no matter what your specific question is. Think about what it is that you need to ask someone for right now. Don't assume that you will get a no. Take the risk to ask. You may get a raise, a donation, a room with an ocean view, a discount, a free sample, a date, time off, or help with the housework. If not, you are no worse off than you were before, and at least others will know that you are willing to ask for what you want. And that alone is a plus. Remember, if you don't ask, the answer will always be no.

> *"The art and science of asking questions is the source of all knowledge."*
>
> Thomas Berger

Final Thoughts—Ask

Asking is a powerful tool to help you move forward in life, personally, professionally, and socially. Don't be afraid to ask. Be confident that the response will be a positive one, but also remain detached from the outcome. Ask with kindness, clarity, and understanding.

My key thoughts are:

- If you want more out of life, you must ask.
- Never assume a no—always ask.
- Examine why you don't want to ask.
- Be specific, ask clearly, and ask the right person.
- Always be grateful when you receive the answer, even if it is a no.
- Offer to do return favors—this balances the giving and taking scales.
- Asking puts the universe on notice to start sending you results.

Intuition

> "The intuitive mind is a sacred gift and the rational mind is a faithful servant. We have created a society that honors the servant and has forgotten the gift."
>
> *Albert Einstein*

Think It

What is intuition? Intuition is the ability to understand something instinctively, without the need for conscious reasoning or proof. Intuition bridges the gap between the conscious and unconscious parts of the mind. Some would call it an unexplainable knowing. Various expressions such as . . .

- by the seat of one's pants
- feel it in one's bones
- follow one's nose
- play it by ear
- listen to one's gut

. . . have been used to describe intuition and instinct. When making the best possible decision for ourselves, our families, and our businesses, we need both intuition and reason.

Many people, however, especially in the business world, don't like to admit that they follow their gut feelings. Others are uncomfortable using intuition as a guidance tool. We don't always trust the messages our intuition sends us, and, therefore, we can diminish our capacity to fully leverage the power of intuition when we need it most.

Intuition provides the highest level of information available to human beings. Intuition taps into a field of knowledge that extends beyond the limits of logic, the individual mind, and the five senses. This field of knowledge contains information that can be extremely useful, even lifesaving, to us. But our *access* to this information is subtle and delicate, so we have a tendency to doubt or ignore it.

Intuition is always at work whether we recognize it or not and whether we honor it or not. It might be telling you things such as the train is going to be late, buy this book, don't go down that street, or your boss really needs this project finished. Have you ever been thinking about someone and they instantly call you or appear from around a corner? This can be a signal from your intuition.

Intuition can break through to people in various ways. Not everyone *hears* their guidance; some people feel it, some see it as a picture, and some just "know." By sharing information with you, your intuition is trying to help you discern more consciously what is needed in the moment in order to make the best decisions possible. Every one of us has an inner voice, a "guide," or a gut instinct, and it has been with us since birth. Some of us have simply learned to listen to and trust it more than others.

When was the last time you actually thought about following the guidance your intuition gave you? It is probably your greatest gift. It can offer you clarity when you are feeling confused, overwhelmed, or simply looking for answers. So learn to pay attention to the little "insignificant" things that you feel or that pop into your mind. Take a moment, check in with that voice or feeling or thought, and see what it might mean. Make this a lifelong habit.

There are various ways by which you can connect to your intuition. You may want to ask yourself some questions and listen to the first answer that jumps into your mind. It might be difficult at first because so many thoughts try to crowd your mind, but allow yourself to be discerning. Over time, you will begin to recognize the difference between a true intuitive feeling and a stray or random thought.

You may find that meditating and clearing your head of mind chatter will make it easier to listen to your intuition. If you haven't meditated before, start with a simple guided meditation. Slowly build up your ability to sit in silence and stillness while gently letting go of intruding thoughts. Intuition speaks to us in silence.

Pay attention to your gut. A gut feeling is your physical response to intuition. If a decision you are about to make is a negative one, you can be sure to feel the discomfort in your stomach region, hence the name "gut feeling."

Being creative and using the right side of your brain is also a good way to tap into your intuition. You might consider singing, dancing, painting, or just allowing yourself to visualize in an imaginative way.

Practicing mindfulness as you go about your day will also be of great benefit. Your intuition isn't loud and is easily drowned out by your rational thoughts. Observe what comes up unexpectedly in your mind. Do you have an unexplained urge to take a certain action or go to a certain place? Follow through.

Look for signs, and be receptive to them. If a book falls off your shelf for no apparent reason, open the book and see if it contains a message you need to hear. Pay attention to coincidences, and make note of images, symbols, words, or other "signs" that appear in your environment. These might be your subconscious trying to communicate with you through intuition.

If in doubt, smile and let go. Sometimes when we are faced with the most difficult decisions, we put so much pressure on ourselves to do what is right that we forget that life is here to be enjoyed and is made up of a series of experiences. No matter what choice we make, there is no right or wrong. The outcome will simply contain the lesson we need to grow as people and to be the best we can be.

Lastly, make sure to fully pay attention to the feelings in your body. Your body will tell you when you may be in danger as well as when you are making the best possible choice in the moment. Your body is a powerful intuitive communicator; it is vital to listen to it. When your intuition shows you that you've found something or someone that is truly right for you, the choice often becomes strangely easy. It feels good; it doesn't feel as if you are forcing it.

> *"You must train your intuition—you must trust the small voice inside you which tells you exactly what to say, what to decide."*
> *Ingrid Bergman*

Feel It

Do you often find yourself struggling to make a decision about something, and you just can't decide? Many of us tend to over-think decisions by using our rational minds. We make a pros and cons list and become extremely analytical. We forget to tap into and trust our intuition. The next time you have a decision to make, why not try this simple exercise?

- Close your eyes. Take a deep breath, and, as you breathe out, let go of any thoughts or worries you've been holding.
- Repeat this a few times to clear the mind chatter.

- Set your intention to be in the present moment, the now.
- See yourself as being in a calm and peaceful place.
- Take a few more deep breaths, and pay attention to your body.
- Notice if there is any tension or a discernible feeling anywhere in your body. Don't try to change it or make it disappear; just notice it.
- What is it communicating to you?
- Place your hand over your heart, and bring to mind someone you love. Listen to the wisdom of your heart. Hear what it is saying about the decision you have to make.
- Observe whatever thoughts or feelings come up. Do not get caught up in the mind by analyzing them.
- Trust that your intuition is guiding you. Ask for discernment. Your answer may be to take some action, to do some research, or to simply wait. Feel good about whatever your intuition is telling you.
- Open your eyes when you feel ready.
- Is there anything you feel encouraged to do right now? If so, then do it. If not, then the time for action is not right yet. Just stay centered in whatever you are presently doing in your life.

If you didn't get your answer right away, be patient and trust that all you need is being provided. Remember, intuitive information often comes when you least expect it. You might feel guided to listen to a radio or TV show later in the day or week and be given the answer there. Or perhaps a magazine or a comment from a friend will contain the answer. Stay open to the guidance of your intuition.

Do It

But let's not stop there. Here are three other ways you can tap into your intuition—that reliable internal voice—and allow its guidance to inform your everyday life:

- Keep a journal. Writing your thoughts and feelings down on paper, even if you think you have little to say, helps the unconscious mind open up. You may find yourself writing words and sentences that don't even make sense to you. Or your words may stir emotional responses rather than intellectual responses. That's fine. In fact, that's great. Allow the process to unfold as it will.
- Switch off your "internal critic." If an inner conversation is taking place, listen to it without judgment and allow it to play out without any fear or ridicule. Be kind to yourself.
- Find or create a quiet place. A comfortable and silent place where you can allow your emotions to flow freely is an essential part of connecting with your intuition. Here, in your quiet place, you may want to create an emotional connection to an object, a color, an aspect of nature, a piece of music, or a work of art—anything that will allow your emotions to flow without rational interference.

By using these three exercises, you will create a new, deeper relationship with your intuition, help clarify that inner voice, and begin to bring instinctual awareness back into your everyday life.

> *"Everyone who wills can hear the inner voice.*
> *It is within everyone."*
>
> *Mahatma Gandhi*

Final Thoughts—Intuition

As you can see, honing your intuition is one of the best gifts you can give yourself. It is a powerful way to help others as well. Allow yourself time to cultivate your inner voice and learn how best to connect with it and use it in your life. Your intuition may present itself in various ways; be open to the signs and signals.

My key thoughts are:

- Notice the quiet inner voice, and recognize it as intuition.
- Pay attention to your gut feelings.
- Pay attention to signs that come up in your environment.
- Connect with silence through meditation and mindfulness.
- Be creative.
- Practice using your intuition daily.

Action

> "Today, many will awaken with a fresh sense
> of inspiration. Why not you?"
>
> Steve Maraboli

Think It

Action can be defined as the process of doing something, typically to achieve an aim. However, in this chapter, I would like to focus on a particular kind of action—namely, inspired action. Inspired action, as its name suggests, is action you take when you feel inspired to do it. Something within you moves you positively and spontaneously toward a specific behavior.

Why is there a difference between action and inspired action? Let's assume you have some goals you would like to accomplish in your life and business. You write a list of objectives, make plans on how to implement them, and start taking the steps to put the actions into play.

At this point, you may begin to "force" the action to happen. That is, you take the action for the sole purpose of following the plan or because you think you should be doing something. Typically, there is little motivation, excitement, or enjoyment from this type of action. It feels like a struggle with few results. You may even lose sight of what your goals are. You will probably find problems cropping up and hindering the process. When you take uninspired action:

- You feel frustrated and overwhelmed. There is so much to do!
- Something is always getting in the way. Things don't seem to be moving ahead.
- You don't want to do it, yet you feel you have to.
- You feel tired and depleted.
- You spend a lot of time trying to figure out what actions to take. You create lists.
- You feel that *you* have to be the one to make it happen and do it all.

Inspired action, on the other hand, is nearly always accompanied by feelings of enthusiasm, joy, excitement, and energy. The impulse to act occurs naturally and at unplanned and unexpected times. Everything just flows without being forced. You feel as if you are in "the zone" and can accomplish more than you ever thought was possible. You tend to work harder, but it doesn't feel like work. It feels as if everything is falling perfectly into place. The process runs smoothly, and a great deal is accomplished in a relatively short timeframe. When you take inspired action:

- You enjoy the process and feel energized by it.
- You make a lot of progress quickly with little effort.
- You forget about time.
- You allow things to happen naturally.
- You find that the action steps make sense with no need to justify them.

Inspired action takes the form of a simple nudge or jolt to take some action. For example, you might suddenly get a desire to drive to the store. You may have no idea why you need to go to the store right now, but something inside is urging you to go. That hunch may lead you closer to accomplishing your goal. You might meet the right person, find the right product, or pick up the right magazine, and any of these might steer you toward realizing your dream.

Is there anything you can do to encourage more inspired action in your life? Start with setting an intention. An intention is different from a goal. A goal is a specific outcome that is accomplished at a particular time *in the future*. An intention has more to do with what you desire to be and accomplish *in the present*. Be clear about your intention; the clearer you are, the better your results.

Allow yourself to follow whatever hunches and desires arise. Listen to your intuition, and if you sense a longing to make a plan of action, then make it. However, if the wish is to go for a walk, read a magazine, or make a phone call, then do that—you never know where your inspired action will take you.

Trust your inspired action. It is leading you down an easier path to achieving your dreams than constant struggle. Try it out and see.

If, for any reason, you currently find yourself in a less-than-inspired situation, start to take baby steps toward inviting inspiration into your life. Break one of your habits, and do something unusual instead. When you go to bed each night, invite inspiration to come in your sleep. Spend a few minutes each day fantasizing about your dreams. Write a list of things you love. Any of these steps can get the inspiration engine churning. Then, when you feel the slightest "nudging" to do something, do it. Inspiration comes to those who act on it.

So long as you can feel the essence of where you are heading and keep taking inspired action to move towards your ultimate calling in life, then you are on the right track to achieve your goals and dreams.

There is no time like the present to start.

"Allow yourself to be inspired. Allow yourself to succeed. Dare to excel."
Vince Dente

Feel It

Inspired action happens when an idea gets holds of you and you feel compelled to do something about it. The key, I believe, to tapping into your own inspiration is to first believe that it exists.

If you believe you have never been inspired, then you must allow yourself to believe it is possible. Look around you at others who lead inspired lives, and see the evidence. It is important to *want* inspiration and to ask for it. Say to yourself, silently or out loud, "I want to be more inspired." Then notice how coincidences, synchronicities, and connections suddenly start to turn up around you. When you notice these, pay attention to the clues and take action. Even if it's a very tiny step. Once you start acting on the small things, you will be inspired to greater and greater actions.

Do you remember a time when you were working on a project that seemed hard and felt as if it took forever to complete? There were endless obstacles along the way, and it felt like a tough challenge? This is what uninspired action feels like.

Can you now think of a time when you were working from an inspired place? I am sure you have had this experience. You were working on a project, and it almost effortlessly completed itself. Flow was constant, and the right people kept turning up at the right time. Close your eyes, and allow yourself to tap back into that feeling. Remember how good it felt.

Place yourself back in that environment emotionally. Feel the enthusiasm, the flow, and the fun. Experience the laughter of your co-workers. Recall how you dealt with any issues or problems that arose during the project. Remember how you focused on the solutions, not the problems, and how answers seemed to appear from nowhere. There was camaraderie, excitement, and enjoyment, and the project was a success.

Write down a list of key moments in your life when you felt you were operating under inspired action. Keep this list handy, and use it as a memory trigger. I encourage you to tap into these memories of inspired action anytime a project gets tough or feels like an endless hurdle.

Compare the feeling of your past inspired action to the way you feel about your current project. With your memories as your guide, imagine how it would feel to be so inspired right now. Notice where your present resistance is coming from. What would it feel like to let go of the resistance? Really imagine the feeling of letting your resistance go. Feel how light you are without the resistance.

As you go to bed tonight, ask for the key to feeling inspired about your present work. Trust that the answer will be delivered.

Do It

Let's imagine you are working on a project at work and it is feeling like a slog. It's arduous and unrewarding, and obstacles keep turning up. You are trying to decide whether or not to take a particular action. Stop for a moment, and ask yourself some simple questions, for example:

- Why am I taking this action?
- How does this action feel?

- Does it seem as if this action will lead to stress or that it will be great fun?
- Do I feel closer to fear or enjoyment?
- What am I afraid will happen if I don't take this action?

By allowing yourself to answer these questions, you will see that you are focusing on the negative emotions such as fear and stress and disapproval that you have attached to the project. You will probably get the project completed, but it will take much longer than if you were in a positive, inspired mindset.

In order to get out of this negative mindset and back into inspired action, I would urge you to do the following:

- If possible, walk away from your desk, and leave the project for at least five minutes. Longer if possible.
- Allow yourself to be re-inspired by looking at projects you or others have completed successfully.
- Get into a feeling of alignment with achievement, success, and believing it is possible.
- Create positive expectations that the process will work.
- Allow yourself to feel good, passionate, and joyful about the project. You can make this choice by letting the resistance go.
- Visualize a positive outcome.
- Deliberately get your happy face on.

"When I'm inspired, I get excited because I can't wait to see what I'll come up with next."
Dolly Parton

Final Thoughts—Action

By taking inspired action, you are aligning with your purpose, vision, passion, and the highest possibilities for your life. Pay attention to your emotions, and notice whether you are in a positive or negative mindset. If negative, look at ways to reconnect and realign with positive vibes to allow inspired action to take place. My key thoughts are:

- Set an intention—"I want to be more inspired."
- Inspired action always feels good, and things happen easily and naturally.
- When inspired, your action steps make sense; there is no need to justify them.
- Trust your inspired action; it is always on track.
- Get yourself into a feeling of alignment with achievement and success.

Your mindset can either squelch action or inspire action.

9

Purpose

"Passion and purpose go hand in hand. When you discover your purpose, you will normally find it's something you're tremendously passionate about."

Steve Pavlina

Think It

Purpose can be defined as one's reason for doing something, one's sense of resolve, or one's overriding intention. In this chapter, we will focus on exploring your *life's* purpose, which encompasses all three of these definitions.

Many of us have no clue as to what we truly want to do in our lives, and when asked the question "What is your life's purpose?" we either stammer and look at our shoes, or else we hurl a small object at the questioner. We don't know the answer. Isn't it odd that when asked the most important question in life, many of us do not have a reply?

We often assume that others know their purpose in life simply because they seem so busy and serious and dedicated. But even though they may be attending a great school, working in a good job, or running their own successful business, this still doesn't mean they know what their purpose is.

Some people find their life purpose easily and early in life; for others, it is a longer and harder struggle; some never find it at all. Perhaps you're a rather pessimistic person who doesn't believe you have a purpose and thinks that life has no meaning. Not believing you have a purpose will not necessarily prevent you from discovering it, but it may take you a longer time than others, and you may find it by default rather than by choice. However, if you are an optimist, you will be excited to find your life's purpose because you recognize the power of purpose to shape your destiny. Which scenario would you prefer?

In order to explore your life's purpose, it is imperative to understand where your passions and talents lie. To do this, you need to clear your mind of all the chatter, the negative thoughts about what you can and cannot do. It doesn't matter what anyone else has previously told you about what you are capable of, or what you may have believed about yourself; now is the time to dive into your deepest desires and discover what makes your heart and soul sing.

Let's look at some soul-searching questions:

- If you had all the money in the world, how would you spend your time?
- What would your perfect day look like? Describe every detail.

- What do you really love to do?
- What really makes your heart sing and sets your soul on fire?
- What do other people repeatedly tell you that you do extremely well?

Delve into these questions, keep your mental judgment filter switched off, and write down whatever comes to mind. You might find you go over and over these questions many times in order to fine-tune your answers.

Once you have these answers ready, you may want to try to gain some glimpses of your childhood wisdom and explore what you loved to do as a child. Allow yourself to connect with your inner child and ask the following questions:

- What brought you enormous joy as a child?
- What were you doing when you totally lost track of time?
- What did your parents have to drag you away from?
- What did you love deep down before you were told to get realistic?

Study the answers to both sets of questions; see where the synergies lie and where is it possible to make connections. Let your creative mind look at the answers fully. Don't worry if you cannot make a synthesis right away; sometimes it helps to sleep on it and allow your subconscious to present the answer to you whenever it is ready.

We are all here for a reason, and not one person on the planet has the same strengths, skills, talents, creativity, and wisdom that you do. You have something exceptional to offer the world, but first you must learn to embrace what your amazing gifts are. Acknowledge and celebrate your own uniqueness while getting in touch with the heartfelt desires you want to fulfill. Somewhere at the intersection of your gifts and your desires is your purpose.

I have found that one of the key obstacles to discovering our life purpose is that we often search for it in the wrong place. What if your life purpose is more about who you *are* than what you *do*? As Steve Pavlina said in the quote at the start of the chapter, "Passion and purpose go hand in hand." By acknowledging what you are passionate about, you are heading in the right direction to uncover your purpose.

> *"Musicians must make music, artists must paint, poets must write if they are to be ultimately be at peace with themselves. What human beings can be, they must be."*
> *Abraham Maslow*

Feel It

Although it is crucial to follow our passions and gifts, one thing we need to acknowledge is that we have limited time. Let's face it; there are only twenty-four hours in a day, and it's important to invest that time wisely in order to help us produce the results we want. There is a third factor that is just as important as passion and talent. That is *values*. Our values help us focus on our true priorities. Values act as a compass to keep us on course every single day so that we are constantly moving closer to our definition of the best life we could possibly live.

Start by writing down a list of your values, the qualities of life that are most important to you. Don't worry about how long the list is or about putting it in any specific order. Here are some examples:

- Happiness
- Love
- Health
- Wealth
- Fun
- Success
- Peace
- Intimacy
- Security
- Adventure
- Learning

The next step is to bring the list down to around five or six values that are most important to you and prioritize your list. Where possible, look at combining values that are closely related, such as fun and adventure.

Now allow yourself to intuitively feel what your number-one value is. Follow that up with the number-two, and so on, until you complete the list. You may want to ask yourself, "If I could only satisfy one of these values, which one would it be?" or "Which of these values is truly the most important to me?" Asking these questions will evoke emotion, and this is important. Allow yourself to truly feel it.

Imagine if you chose security as your number-one priority. Although this may make you feel more confident and safe about your life, what emotions does this choice bring up? If you were to focus mainly on security, would you feel you were missing out on the fun and adventure in life? It is important to really let yourself feel and explore such emotions before completing the list.

Once the list is finished, review it. You will be easily able to identify what drives you in fulfilling your life. Everybody's path is different. For example, if you were to choose success as number one, security as number two, and learning as number three, your focus should probably be on your career. If, however, you chose peace, happiness, and love as your values, you might want to focus on relationships and family rather than career success.

Paying attention to your values will help guide you to answering the following questions:

- What kind of work feels most rewarding to you?
- What causes are you drawn to supporting?
- What are the things you do that make you feel fulfilled?
- What brings meaning to your life?

Looking carefully at your values, gifts, and passions *will* bring your life's purpose into focus, whether that happens quickly and obviously or slowly and intuitively.

Do It

Having helped many clients find their purpose through their passion, I would like to share some of the helpful tools I use.

Create a Mission Statement

Once you have assessed your values, gifts, and passions, create a written mission statement about yourself. This can help you hone in on your life's purpose even more accurately. Your mission statement should focus on the legacy you feel you want to create. It will help people, including yourself, understand who and what you stand for. First re-read your values list and then try out the following exercise:

- Write "What is my true purpose in life?" on a blank sheet of paper.
- Write an answer, any answer that pops into your head; phrases and incomplete sentences are fine.
- Try again with a different answer.
- Keep writing all answers possible until you feel you have nothing more to write.
- Review your responses. One of them will elicit more emotion than the others; you may even cry when you read it.

This unique answer will resonate with you, and you will have found your purpose. Now spend some time polishing it up until you feel the phrasing is just right.

By synthesizing your gifts, passions, and values together in a committed mission statement, you can now use this statement as a daily reminder to help you *become* that purpose. As an example, here is my mission statement: "My mission is to maximize my clients' and readers' potential, with integrity, through inspiration, empowerment, and love."

Make a Vision Board

A vision board is probably one of the best visualization tools you can create to help you harness anything you want in life. It represents your dreams, your goals, and your ideal life. The mind responds strongly to visual stimulation. Mental pictures amplify our emotions and activate the universal law of attraction.

Here is a simple process to create your own vision board:

- Find pictures that represent or symbolize the experiences, feelings, people, circumstances, and possessions you want to attract into your life. These can be cutouts from magazines, printouts from the Internet, personal photos, etc. Choose images that inspire you and make you feel good.
- Place and arrange them on the board. Have fun during the process, and be creative with the arrangement.

- Use words, too, and make sure they speak to you.
- Place a happy, feel-good picture of yourself on the board.
- Keep the board neat, not cluttered or chaotic.
- Make sure it captures your purpose, your ideal future.

Once you have finished the vision board, place it somewhere in your home where you will see it often and feel the inspiration it provides to you. You can also consider taking a photo of it and placing it on your smart phone or computer. When you achieve goals, mark them in some way. This will bring you closer to living your purpose.

Start Doing What You Love
We often get wrapped up in the expectations we set for ourselves. We focus on to-do lists and details instead of what is important. Ask yourself these questions:

- What do you love to do?
- What makes you smile?
- If money were limitless, what would you be doing today?

When you do something you really love, you always give it your all. Maybe it's time to prove that to yourself.

"The pen that writes your life story must be held in your own hand."

Irene C. Kassorla

Final Thoughts—Purpose

By focusing on our values, gifts, and passions, it is possible to truly find our life's purpose. Purpose gives us direction and meaning so that we may live the best life possible for ourselves and our families. Everyone has a unique set of talents and gifts to share with the world, and by using yours, you will feel more fulfilled in whatever you choose to do.

My key thoughts are:

- Connect with your inner child.
- Find your passion.
- Understand your values.
- Do what you love.
- Create a mission statement about yourself.
- Use a vision board to identify and focus on your life purpose.

10

Happiness

> "I, not events, have the power to make me happy or unhappy today. I can choose which it shall be. Yesterday is dead, tomorrow hasn't arrived yet. I have just one day, today, and I'm going to be happy in it."
>
> Groucho Marx

Think It

Happiness is generally defined as a state of well-being characterized by positive emotions ranging from contentment and optimism to intense joy. Some philosophers and religious thinkers expand the definition to include living a good life rather than simply attaining a positive emotional state.

Most of us agree that happiness is definitely worth pursuing, but how many of us explore what it truly means to us personally? Some of us look at other people and decide that they must be happy because they have a big house, a nice car, a large bank balance, great friends, and/or a nice-looking family. Others of us believe that happiness can only be achieved through having no possessions or relationships at all. One way or another, we equate happiness with circumstances.

We therefore assume that *our own* circumstances—for example, where we live, what we own, and what we earn—have a big effect on how happy *we* are. Have you ever said to yourself, for instance, I'll be happy when . . .

- I get that perfect job.
- I meet my soul mate.
- I get a promotion at work.
- I have *X* amount of money in the bank.
- I have a fit body?

By putting a condition on our happiness, we are unconsciously deferring happiness until an imaginary date in the future when we hope that condition will be met. But by doing this—by believing that things, people, and circumstances will make us happy—we are simply kidding ourselves. Circumstances tend to have less impact on happiness than most of us think. Each of us is unique, and how happy we are depends on many different factors, including our genes, our psychological makeup, and our approach to life. Have you ever had the experience of spending years chasing a goal you thought would make you happy only to discover, fifteen minutes after you achieved it, that this was a pure illusion? This is where misery and depression can set in, causing a downward emotional spiral.

I believe that happiness is an inside job. We are happy when we *decide* to be. Only then and at no other time. Happiness is generated by our attitudes, our personal values, and our sense of purpose. But here's the fun part: this puts happiness completely in our own hands. We don't have to wait until the circumstances are perfect. We have a brilliant opportunity to make ourselves and others happier by the actions we choose to take and the way we approach our lives.

By getting out of our heads and into our hearts, we can allow ourselves to feel happier *right now*. We can build small changes into our day—such as getting ten minutes of fresh air, helping someone else, smiling more, spending a bit more time with people we love, or simply listening to music—to raise our happiness level rather than wait for circumstances to change.

Only you can make you happy. Once you recognize that external factors do not drive your happiness, you place yourself back in the driver's seat. I see it as being happy for no apparent reason. This doesn't mean denying negative feelings. It means allowing yourself to *have* a negative emotion such as fear, anger, worry, or sadness but at the same time permitting yourself to experience an overall sense of well-being, calmness, and peace—allowing your inner happiness to still be present.

Think of it a little like your heating thermostat. If you set your inner "temperature" daily to happiness, you can actually live *from* happiness rather than *for* happiness. You can stop expecting to extract happiness from people and things. By having an attitude of happiness-no-matter-what, nothing will shake you from a place of emotional strength.

By accepting personal responsibility for our own happiness, we can transform our friendships and love relationships. Many of us fall into the trap of wanting others to act in a specific way to make us happy. If they step outside those parameters, we tend to get upset and blame *them* for causing our unhappiness. However, in deep, honest, and mature relationships, we are individually responsible for our own happiness. We can then allow ourselves to share and grow that happiness together. Relationships in which both parties bring their own happiness to the table are free of jealousy, blame, neediness, and bitterness.

> *"Very little is needed to make a happy life; it is*
> *all within yourself, in your way of thinking."*
> Marcus Aurelius Antoninus

Feel It

What is it you have been telling yourself that you need to do, or be, in order to be happy? Maybe it is a relationship, a job, a home, or a family. Whatever it is, write it down. Then look at your list. How do you feel when you read it? Do you really want to give your power of happiness to these things or people? I trust by now you are saying no.

What I urge you to remember is that you can still want and have all the things on your list, but you don't need to make your happiness dependent on them. Let's look at how you can bring that awareness into play.

Sometimes you may not recognize the language you use in your daily conversations and how it can adversely affect your state of mind. For example, you may catch yourself thinking or saying, "If only . . . X would happen, then I'd be happy." When you do this, stop, take a breath, and say to yourself, "No, I choose to be happy anyway."

Notice where you are putting your emotional focus; is it on the *lack* of things you are striving for or on the *presence* of all the things you have in your life already? I know it sounds simple, but, in my experience, this is a choice. And when we flip from lack-consciousness to presence-consciousness, we immediately raise our happiness thermostat.

Your emotions are like the GPS for your soul; their primary function is to help you travel from where you are to wherever you want to be. Happiness is a perfect example of this. Imagine waking up in the morning and feeling good no matter what—holding yourself fully and deeply in a place of joy and happiness. Try to put yourself in this state right now. Feel the excitement run through your body. Feel the adrenal flow. Focus on being present in the moment and allowing yourself to just be happy. You are now aligned with your soul and in a great place. Why not start each and every day with such happiness vibes?

By allowing yourself to choose the state of happiness, feel it, and believe it, you can remain happy even if you have a challenging day. Even if things do go wrong, you can approach it from a perspective of "This does not mean I am required to feel unhappy." You will then be much better equipped to deal with whatever challenge is facing you at that moment.

From time to time, you might slip back into the old habit of assigning your happiness to things or people. That's OK; we all do it. It's part of learning a new practice. When you catch yourself doing this, simply regroup and check in with your emotions. Acknowledge whatever you are feeling; then remind yourself that your happiness is your choice and your responsibility. Reset your inner thermostat to happiness. In time, this will become an automatic response.

Do It

To tap into the happiness mindset, you might want to consider doing some or all of the following:

Help Others

By helping others, we focus beyond ourselves, allowing us to be more connected to the world at large. This takes us out of "me-only" thinking and automatically raises our vibration. For example, you can donate your time and energy at local charities, community clubs, or organized charity events. Who knows—you might even make some new friends who are upbeat, generous people.

Focus on Positives

Focusing your attention on the positive aspects of any situation will help you enjoy the moment and bolster your happiness level in the here and now.

Be Kind

Practice random acts of kindness on a daily or weekly basis, whether for friends, colleagues, family members, or complete strangers. Pay the toll for the car behind you, buy the security guard at your office a coffee, leave a gift on your neighbor's doorstep.

Be Present

Cut down on your use of technology and engage with people around you. Yes, those living, breathing *Homo sapiens*!

Say "Thank You"

Say a simple but sincere "thank you" for every small act and gesture, especially those that usually go unheralded.

Focus on Your Strengths

Whether you're engaged in work or a hobby, focus on developing your strengths rather than correcting your flaws and weaknesses.

Keep a Gratitude Journal

Writing a gratitude journal daily will help yourself focus on the great things that are present in your life rather than the things that are missing. And when "negative" events happen, you will be able to learn from them.

Happiness Experiment

For one day, why not consider doing some, or all, of the suggestions above and allowing yourself to tap into your happiness mindset? Keep a record of your emotions throughout the day, and, no matter what challenge or obstacles come up, notice how happy you were or were not able to be. What did you learn from this?

This exercise will help you learn how to be in control of your own happiness and recognize it as an inside job.

"Happiness depends upon ourselves."
Aristotle

Final Thoughts—Happiness

It can be difficult to acknowledge that our happiness is our own responsibility, but once we recognize this and practice it, we realize that we are in the driver's seat toward a more fulfilled life. Start your day from a place of happiness, and, when challenges arise, learn from them and acknowledge that they cannot impact your happiness factor.

My key thoughts are:

- Happiness is an inside job.
- Choose to be happy daily.
- Delete "if only" from your vocabulary.
- You can still be happy even if things go wrong.
- Help others, focus on positives, and be kind.
- Be grateful for what you have.

Love

"You can search throughout the entire universe for someone who is more deserving of your love and affection than you are yourself, and that person is not to be found anywhere. You yourself, as much as anybody in the entire universe, deserve your love and affection."

Author Unknown
(sometimes attributed to Buddha)

Think It

What is love? I am sure you are familiar with the Beatles song "All You Need Is Love," but do you truly love yourself? Our focus in this chapter will be on self-love because I believe that loving yourself is the foundation stone on which all loving relationships are built.

You deserve to be loved not only by those around you but by the most important person in your life—you. There is no other person in the world like you. You are unique and extraordinary. Self-love is about accepting and loving yourself as you are, meeting your own needs, allowing yourself to feel and think whatever you feel and think, and seeing yourself as good, worthy, valuable, and deserving of love and happiness. Self-love means showing up in the world as *you* and letting yourself be seen and felt that way by others.

Most of us don't fully love ourselves. Early childhood experiences; relationships with peers, siblings, friends, and colleagues; and even our culture may have damaged our sense of self-love. Understanding these factors can help you uncover why you adopted a feeling of unworthiness of love in the first place and see how you might manage your thoughts and feeling from a different perspective.

Choosing self-love means being brave enough to make the choices that bring you more happiness even when things seem tough and difficult. Most of us get caught up in our ego, which is driven by fear more than love. We allow the ego to control us and create unnecessary suffering. This suffering may express itself as shame, despair, anxiety, self-doubt, depression, anger, confusion, and/or feelings that we are not good enough.

But what if all we had to do was surrender to our own self-love? Having the faith to surrender to self-love allows us to see love as abundance, prosperity, happiness, peace, great relationships, and more. So how do we do it?

Say "I love you," and smile when you look at yourself in the mirror. When you look in the mirror, do you generally notice all the things you don't like? Do you wish you were slimmer, more beautiful, and healthier? How would life be different if you could look in the mirror with acceptance, joy, and love? You might feel a little silly by saying "I love you" and smiling at your own image. You might not believe yourself at first, but it's a start to creating a healthier judgment of yourself. Try it out for a week, and notice how different you feel.

Lose the negative self-talk. What you say in your mind goes a long way toward determining how you feel about who you are. Pay attention to what you say about yourself. Note the doubts, fears, and negative expressions. Be kind to yourself, and learn to develop better self-talk. This starts with listening to what you are saying about yourself each day. Monitor your self-talk, and, if you need to, write it down.

Stop comparing yourself to others. There is only one you. You are one of a kind. No one else can do a better job of being you than you. If you compare yourself to others, you will often end up judging yourself negatively.

Notice what drains you. You need to protect your self-love against being drained by people and situations around you. Some people, for example, are energy vampires, sucking the positivity from you with their negative mindset. Notice what situations you might be putting up with that aren't benefitting you. What boundaries can you set? What changes can you make in order to take your power back?

Learn to say "no." In wanting to help and please others, we often walk around with a "yes" sign on our heads.

It is important not to feel obliged to say yes. Remember, you have a choice about what you agree to do. If you need more time to decide whether you should give a yes or a no, just tell the other person you will get back to them. There are only twenty-four hours in each day, and it is important to leave some time for you.

Create a self-love ritual every day. Decide what you need to bring into your daily routine to help you focus on loving yourself more. This can be anything from creating time for a cherished hobby to doing activities that raise your energy level to reading an uplifting or inspiring book. Choose what you feel is needed in your life right now.

Other ideas to consider when growing your self-love are:

- Find time to connect with yourself and just *be*.
- Do something you are good at.
- Be the best version of you.

All of the above activities will help you focus on creating a happier relationship with yourself. The self-awareness you gain will lead to healthier and more realistic expectations of friendships and love relationships. You will begin to look at all relationships with a different set of eyes. By fully loving yourself, you will be in a much stronger position to love another. Your non-judgment of yourself will empower you to be more accepting and appreciative of the other person. Your ability to love yourself will also enable you to *accept* love from others. This, in turn, will lead to a greater abundance of love, fulfillment, and joy in all of your relationships.

> *"To love yourself right now, just as you are, is to give yourself heaven. Don't wait until you die. If you wait, you die now. If you love, you live now."*
>
> Alan Cohen

Feel It

Let's try a simple visualization exercise to help you focus on feeling self-love. Imagine it is the last day of your life. Ask yourself, "Did I live, love, and matter?" I know this can be a very challenging and poignant question. As you consider your answer, think about these questions as well:

- What overall feeling do you get when you think about your life? Let the positives and negatives flash before you.
- Did you do the things you really wanted to do?
- What were your greatest achievements and accolades?
- Was it a fun and enjoyable life?
- Did you live a healthy life? How did you look after yourself? What foods did you love? What exercise and fitness regimen was important to you? What other factors contributed to your health? How did your body feel?

- Did you love yourself enough? Did you love your work and friends? Did you love your spouse and children?
- Did you practice acceptance and tolerance in these relationships?
- Did you show and tell the people close to you that you loved them?
- Did you have fun together?
- Did you tell them, "You're the best"?
- Did you respect them?
- How did you really feel about these relationships?
- Then ask yourself, "Do I feel I have done the best I could?"

These questions will help you see what thoughts and behaviors you can change in your life right now, which will, in turn, allow you to direct your destiny.

Now picture yourself again in your final day of life. Allow yourself to feel the love of all those people who are by your bedside. Ask yourself what truly matters most. Was it the job, the accolades, the things that you accumulated over the years? I think you will see that the most important aspect of life is to love and be loved. But it all starts with you. Do you love *yourself* enough?

Can you do something for yourself every day, something that makes you happy and feel alive? Can you then *feel* the love for yourself and show it in your face, your eyes, and your smile to everyone who graces your path in life? Love is inside of you. Love is who you are on a soul level. Love is your natural state.

Do It

We can all be our own worst critics, and this self-criticism can really eat away at our love for ourselves. Here's a tip to consider; I call it the two-for-one rule. Whenever you hear yourself making a self-critical comment, immediately follow it up with two compliments (ideally but not necessarily related to the criticism). Through practice, you will learn to turn off the negative voice in your head for good.

Remind yourself every day that you are enough! From the moment you were born, you were enough, and you will be enough every second of your entire life. There is no need to be judged by yourself or others on the basis of how you look, what you earn, what you drive, or what you have achieved. Accept that your essential value comes from simply being you.

Be kind and gentle with yourself. Go softly. Give yourself space to learn and make mistakes. Your relationship with yourself is no different from any other relationship. Show some kindness to yourself daily. Give yourself what you need. If you need time alone, acknowledge it, set your boundaries, and learn to say no to others. Ask yourself what else you might need. Is it security, adventure, or just time out? Focus on meeting your own needs in whatever way is required. Set time aside to be with yourself, to enjoy things that feel good to you. This might mean watching a movie, reading a book, taking an exercise class, or just cooking a meal. Learn how to be happy in your own company.

Lastly, appreciate and love your own qualities. Take time to acknowledge what you appreciate and love about yourself. Be your own best friend.

> *"Whatever you are doing, love yourself for doing it. Whatever you are feeling, love yourself for feeling it."*
>
> Thaddeus Golas

Final Thoughts—Love

Loving yourself is one of the most important gifts you can give yourself. There is no one else like you in this world, and you deserve to be appreciated. Although practicing self-love may be difficult, especially at times when you face serious challenges, doing so will empower you to live a joyous life in which your ideas, desires, and passions are honored. It will also give you the foundation upon which to build mature and loving relationships with others. Today is the day to launch a lifelong campaign of self-love. My key thoughts are:

- Tell yourself you are good enough.
- Always love yourself (mind, body, and spirit).
- Be responsible for your actions (choose well).
- Pay attention to your self-talk.
- Feed your passions and talents.
- Stop comparing yourself to others.
- Give and share love.

Gratitude

"If the only prayer you said in your whole life was, 'thank you,' that would suffice."
                                                    Meister Eckhart

Think It

Gratitude is the new attitude to have in everyday life. By simply acknowledging all the things we are grateful for, we become more aware of the gifts we have received, which brings even more gifts to us, which in turn brings more thankfulness into our lives. Gratitude creates a virtual cycle of ever-expanding benefits.

In my life, I am so grateful for all the lessons that have popped up along the way—the struggles I had with my education that taught me how to be responsible for my own learning; the failed relationships that taught me to love myself and to look at my own needs and desires instead of always being there for someone else; the blows to my ego that taught me to no longer seek approval from others in life or in business. Every "negative" situation has a blessing wrapped up in it. The trick is to be open to the blessings and grateful for the challenges.

I have noticed something interesting. Often the people who look for gratitude the most are those who practice it the least. How about you? Are you always looking for gratitude yet not practicing it? Think about how you can change your attitude toward gratitude to make a difference in your life today.

I practice gratitude every evening before I go to sleep. This practice, perhaps more than any other technique I employ, has transformed my life for the better. I take my gratitude journal from the bedside drawer, and, no matter how tired I am, I write something. Sometimes it is only one line; other times it is pages and pages. The mere act of being thankful creates an incredibly peaceful and loving feeling before going to sleep.

The most important aspect of gratitude is to give thanks for what you already have. So many people take good health, a job, a home, good friends, and family for granted, and they appear to be on a continual search for something else. Imagine how you would feel if everyone and everything you had were suddenly taken away from you. Think about how much you would give to have it all back and how thankful you would feel if it were returned to you. Give thanks every day with that kind of intensity.

Recent scientific and psychological studies about happiness universally confirm that people who are thankful are happier, healthier, less depressed, and less stressed than others. They also have better relationships and make greater progress toward achieving their personal goals.

Do you want to feel better? Are you ready to make one simple change in your life and be more thankful?

Why not explore a day of gratitude? Just a day for starters. Let's start with your morning. Whom do you share it with? What did you eat for breakfast? Think about the fact that many people in the world do not have fresh, wholesome food to eat or a partner to share it with. What about the bus driver or train conductor who showed up on time to get you to work? Would a word of appreciation be in order? Did you grab a coffee on the way into the office? Did you think about the person who grew the coffee beans or the coffee roaster who carefully roasted them till they were just right? How did you respond to the person who served you?

If you were at the office or in a business meeting, did you show any gratitude to the secretary, the other attendees, or even just your colleagues who share the office with you? Were you simply too busy to even acknowledge them? A simple statement like "Jennifer, I just want you to know how much I appreciate what you do every day" can change someone's entire day and can even transform a relationship.

Even the simple manners of please and thank you, when spoken sincerely, can kindle a warm feeling of gratitude in both the giver and the receiver. Small rituals such as offering thanks for our food can remind us to keep gratitude alive in our lives. Even if you are not a religious believer, what have you got to lose by blessing your meal before eating it?

Thankfulness can lead to wonderful feelings of love, appreciation, generosity, and compassion, which can further open our hearts and help rewire our brains to fire in more positive patterns.

Gratitude will make you a better husband/wife, mother/father, daughter/son, and a much happier, more positive, and more productive person. It will even make you a better businessperson. More and more, we are learning that people buy with their hearts, so why not show your customers appreciation? Why not think of gratitude as a new form of customer service?

The more grateful you feel, the more you notice the kind things that others do for you. These serve as reminders for you to do similar things for others.

To instantly trigger more gratitude in your life:

- Instead of looking at what you don't have, look at what you do have.
- When you face a big challenge, be grateful for it.
- Instead of complaining about your kids, be grateful for them.
- Instead of criticizing your partner/husband or wife, express gratitude. (This one act alone could save ten million marriages a year!)
- Imagine how you would feel about your life if you only had one day left to live. Would you then appreciate everything you have? Why not do so now?

- When you are having a tough moment or day, stop and make a gratitude list.

Give thanks for what you have in your life, and see how great a day today really is!

> *"Let us be grateful to people who make us happy; they are the charming gardeners who make our souls blossom."*
>
> Marcel Proust

Feel It

"What am I grateful for right now?" Imagine asking yourself this question several times a day. How do you think it would make you feel?

To hone in on this feeling, let's start with a very simple exercise. Take a blank piece of paper and a pen, and start to write your wish list—all the things you think are missing in your life: the needs, wants, and desires. Keep going until you feel you have exhausted the list. Now look at the list, and notice how you feel.

Put the list aside. Take a new piece of paper, and start writing the things you are grateful for right now, today. List things like your home, your friends, the smile from the bus driver, the coin you found on the street, the song you heard on the radio that made you remember a happy moment in your life, the phone call from your mother, the text from your sister, your partner who always brings your flowers, your children, your books—just keep the flow of writing going. Allow yourself to just feel the flow of gratitude. Be emotive, and acknowledge the feelings in your heart, your solar plexus, and the rest of your body.

Now look at the items on your first list, and strike off the items that no longer feel needed or desired. How do you feel now? What feels different from before?

Do It

You might also want to consider doing some of these action-oriented gratitude exercises and see how they make you feel:

- Write a thank-you letter to someone in your life, and consider delivering it in person.
- Make a gratitude vision board or use Pinterest .com to create images of people and things you are grateful for in your life.
- Create a gratitude jar, and add your gratitude notes to it every day. At the end of the year, reread the notes and relive the memories.
- Use the simple manners your parents taught you, such as please and thank you, and do it with fresh sincerity.
- Smile. A smile is an amazing gift to another person, and it costs you nothing to give. See how you feel when they smile back.

- Think about what you might be able to do for a friend to help them. Reach out, and make that offer.
- Find satisfaction in the gifts you already possess. (Almost half the world's people live on a few dollars a day.)
- Lastly, before you go to sleep each night, why not give thanks in a journal or at least in your mind and your heart for the truly wonderful things you have in your life today? Always pick at least three things that you are grateful for.

Remember, if you feel gratitude and don't express it, it is a little like wrapping a present and not giving it. So say the words, and take the actions! We all love to be around grateful people. We feel their positivity, and that helps us feel and act more grateful, too.

> *"Develop an attitude of gratitude, and give thanks for everything that happens to you, knowing that every step forward is a step toward achieving something bigger and better than your current situation."*
>
> *Brian Tracy*

Final Thoughts—Gratitude

Gratitude is an amazing tool to help you change your life because it is so extremely simple and easy to practice. It will help you focus on the benefits you already have and attract even more benefits to you. It will also allow you to focus more fully on the present moment. There is no doubt in my mind that a few simple daily acts of gratitude will have a profound effect on your life.

My key thoughts are:

- Keep a daily gratitude journal.
- Express gratitude always.
- See gratitude in everything (what's right, not wrong).
- Catch people in the act of doing a good job, and tell them.
- Cultivate a grateful heart.
- Write thank-you notes.
- Give thanks to yourself.

Afterword

Well done. You have finished the book.

I truly hope you have enjoyed reading it and have picked up some ideas that can help you play the game of life more effectively and enjoyably. I would encourage you to share the book with your friends and family. Tell them how it has helped and guided you along the way. Get together with your friends and have a "*12 Words*" night once or twice a month. Learn and grow from each other in the process.

Share the ideas with your children, too. Help them understand that life is not as complicated as we think it is, and that they should have fun and play with it! Come back and tell me your stories. I want to know how the book has impacted your life, and what you have done differently as a result of reading it. Tell me the whys and hows.

This is your journey. Life whizzes by so fast, and before you know it, it's over. So I want you to wake up every day feeling inspired, excited, empowered, and motivated in whatever you do. I want you to have fun and really make a difference in your world with your friends and family by your side.

I love the phrase "Live each day as if it were your last." Embrace this thought, and allow yourself to reach for your dreams today rather than putting them off till tomorrow. Focus on the joys in life, and understand the importance of Think It—Feel It—Do It. Once more, the 12 Words are:

- Embrace **Change**
- Let **Fear** go
- Be **Courage**ous
- Always **Believe**
- **Trust**
- **Ask**
- Use your **Intuition**
- Practice **Inspired Action**
- Live your **Purpose**
- Be **Happy**
- **Love, Love, Love**
- And always give **Gratitude**

These are 12 Words for life!

Acknowledgments

Thank you.

I could not have written this book without the support of so many people. In some way you have all touched my life and helped me on my path. I am a great believer that people come into our lives for a reason—whether it be for only a season or for a lifetime—and I also think that every person is a reflection of ourselves and helps us uncover what we need to learn.

My greatest thanks go out to . . .

My dear friend Edward, for his love and friendship, his invaluable advice, and his tireless commitment and guidance in supporting my vision.

My amazing sister and best friend Jackie, for her unconditional love; she constantly reminds me this is what I was born to do.

The rest of my family and friends, for simply loving me as I am.

Dr. James Rouse, for his inspiration and encouragement, and for believing in me.

My wonderful publishers, Brown Books Publishing Group, who have succeeded in the face of adversity with challenges on timelines, locations, and languages that I have requested for this book. I thank them for understanding that this is a movement, a daily practice, and a way to live life.

And lastly to you, dear reader, for choosing this book no matter what the reason was—for allowing yourself to learn, to grow, to share, and, most of all, to accept this book as a tool to guide you on the emotional journey of life. Keep up your amazing work by living a truly authentic and joyful life!

About the Author

Shirley Palmer is the CEO and Founder of Shirley Palmer International Ltd (London) and Shirley Palmer International LLC (Los Angeles). Her business focuses on mindset and leadership. She is a sought-after mindset master, transformational coach, corporate trainer, and speaker. She is passionate about life and is creating a legacy to make a difference in this world while educating, empowering, and inspiring people to achieve their goals in all aspects of their lives.

With over thirty years' experience in business (eighteen in private equity and the last eight in personal and business development), Shirley helps others to reach their maximum potential. She has worked with business leadership experts Robin Sharma and Ali Brown, and she is a member of the Association for Professional Coaches, Trainers, and Consultants. Shirley has the skills to help you build towards present and future success.

Shirley is fervent about sharing knowledge and often speaks on the subjects of life, health, and business. She has contributed as a guest to various radio programs and podcasts. She works with CEOs, entrepreneurs, leaders, luminaries, and visionary thinkers, and she is often described as being dynamic, passionate, sassy, practical, personable, and supportive. Shirley believes that life is as simple as her trademark phrase "Think It, Feel It, and Do It™" and lives her life daily from this powerful place of inspiration!

www.ShirleyPalmer.com